Armstrong's Job Evaluation Handbook

Armstrong's Job Evaluation Handbook

A guide to achieving fairness and transparency in pay and reward

Michael Armstrong

KoganPage

First published in Great Britain and the United States in 2018 by Kogan Page Limited

2nd Floor, 45 Gee Street	c/o Martin P Hill Consulting	4737/23 Ansari Road
London	122 W 27th St, 10th Floor	Daryaganj
EC1V 3RS	New York NY 10001	New Delhi 110002
United Kingdom	USA	India

www.koganpage.com

ISBN   978 0 7494 8242 8
E-ISBN 978 0 7494 8243 5

British Library Cataloguing-in-Publication Data

A CIP record for this book is available from the British Library.

Library of Congress Cataloging-in-Publication Data

Names: Armstrong, Michael, 1928- author.
Title: Armstrong's job evaluation handbook : a guide to achieving fairness
    and transparency in pay and reward / Michael Armstrong.
Description: 1st Edition. | New York : Kogan Page Ltd, [2018] | Includes
    index.
Identifiers: LCCN 2017050322 (print) | LCCN 2018002125 (ebook) | ISBN
    9780749482435 (ebook) | ISBN 9780749482428 (pbk.) | ISBN 9780749481235
    (eISBN)
Subjects: LCSH: Job evaluation.
Classification: LCC HF5549.5.J62 (ebook) | LCC HF5549.5.J62 A75 2018 (print)
    | DDC 658.3/06–dc23
LC record available at https://lccn.loc.gov/2017050322

Typeset by Integra Software Services, Pondicherry
Print production managed by Jellyfish
Printed and bound in Great Britain by CPI Group (UK) Ltd, Croydon CR0 4YY

CONTENTS

Introduction 1

PART ONE The process of job evaluation 3

01   Job evaluation fundamentals 5

Job evaluation defined 5
Purpose of job evaluation 5
The meaning of value 6
Features of job evaluation 8
The basis of job evaluation methodology 10
Market pricing 11
References 12

02   Job evaluation methodology 13

Formal approaches to job evaluation 13
Combined approaches 18
Ready-made and tailor-made schemes 19
Informal approaches to job evaluation 20
Computer-aided job evaluation 20
Use of schemes 25
Reference 25

03   Reviewing job evaluation 27

Formal job evaluation schemes 27
Informal approach 29
Extreme market pricing 29
Decide whether to retain, modify or replace 29
Define objectives 33

Specification 33
Reference 34

04   Choice of approach 35

Extreme market pricing? 35
Formal or informal? 36
What type of formal job evaluation scheme? 38
Reference 43

05   Developing job evaluation 45

The development programme 45
Practical guidance 51
Procedures and policies 55
Reference 58

06   Job analysis 59

Job descriptions 59
Structured interviews 59
Written questionnaire 65
Computer-aided analysis 66
The parties involved in job analysis 66

PART TWO Job evaluation schemes and market
pricing 69

07   Point-factor rating 71

Methodology 71
Designing a point-factor job evaluation scheme 76
Examples 89
References 97

08   Matching 99

Job-to-grade analytical matching 99
Job-to-job analytical matching 100
Non-analytical matching 100

Developing a matching scheme 101
Examples 122

09   Levelling 133

Levelling defined 133
Earlier approaches to levelling 134
The decision-making accountability (DMA) approach 137
References 139

10   Market pricing 141

Applications of market pricing 142
Requirements for effective market rate analysis 143
The process of market analysis 145
Limitations of market pricing 150
References 153

PART THREE Applications of job evaluation 155

11   Developing grade and pay structures 157

Grade and pay structures 157
Grade structures 157
Designing grade structures 159
Pay structures 162
Developing pay structures 162
References 167

12   Equal pay 169

Equal pay law in the UK 170
Defending an equal pay claim in the UK 171
Managing the risk of equal pay claims 172
Equal pay reviews and job evaluation 174
Reference 176

PART FOUR The practice of job evaluation 177

13   Maintaining job evaluation 179

Advice on maintaining job evaluation 179
Reference 182

14   Issues and trends in job evaluation 183

Issues 183
Trends 184
References 186

Appendices 187
    A Job evaluation glossary 187
    B Point-factor job evaluation scheme 189
    C Example of a job questionnaire 192
Index 197

Introduction

As defined by ACAS (2014), 'Job evaluation is a method of determining on a systematic basis the relative importance of a number of different jobs.' ACAS also noted that, 'A job evaluation scheme is a way of systematically assessing individual jobs objectively, while avoiding prejudice or discrimination.'

This book is largely about formal methods of comparing the value of jobs to assess their relative value to the organization (internal relativities). A distinction is made between formal job evaluation schemes such as point-factor rating, analytical matching and levelling, which are solely concerned with internal relativities, and market pricing, which is concerned with ensuring as far as possible that internal pay rates are competitive by comparing them with those in other organizations (external relativities). In its extreme form, market pricing is used alone without any attempt to assess internal relativities through a formal job evaluation system. In the United States, but not in this book, it is classified as a job evaluation process.

Although the focus is on formal job evaluation schemes it is recognized that evaluation takes place every time a decision is made on how much a job is worth on the basis of broad comparisons with other jobs internally or information on the rates paid for similar jobs by outside organizations (market rate comparisons). Such informal approaches are also considered in this book.

Formal job evaluation schemes attracted a lot of criticism in the 1980s and '90s mainly on the grounds that they were rigid, bureaucratic, perpetuated unnecessarily extended hierarchies and ignored market rate considerations. Yet, as the Institute for Employment Studies (Brown et al, 2016) commented on the basis of extensive research: 'Job evaluation seems to be alive and well in UK organizations.' XpertHR's 2013 job evaluation survey revealed that 71 per cent of UK organizations used a job evaluation scheme and 76 per cent of the respondents to the 2017 e-reward survey had one. But, as mentioned in the final chapter of this book on issues and trends, considerable changes have been taking place recently in approaches to job evaluation, with less reliance being placed on traditional point-factor schemes.

The book is divided into the following parts:

Part 1 deals with the fundamental characteristics of job evaluation, its methodology, approaches to reviewing and introducing job evaluation schemes and the basic technique of job analysis.

Part 2 describes the three main formal job evaluation schemes: point-factor rating, matching and levelling. It also covers market pricing.

Part 3 is concerned with applications of job evaluation in the areas of grade and pay structure design.

Part 4 deals with the practice of job evaluation – maintaining job evaluation schemes and an analysis of issues and trends.

References

ACAS (2014) *Job Evaluation: Considerations and risk*, London, ACAS

Brown, D, Bevan, S and Rickard, C (2016) A review of pay comparability methodologies, Institute for Employment Studies [Online] https://www.gov.uk/government/publications/a-review-of-pay-comparability-methodologies [accessed 1 May 2017]

e-reward (2017) *Job Evaluation Survey*, Stockport, e-reward

XpertHR (2013) How to select, devise, and use a job evaluation scheme [Online] http://www.xperthr.co.uk/how-to/how-to-select-devise-and-use-a-job-evaluation-scheme/155642 [accessed 28 September 2017]

PART ONE
The process of job evaluation

Job evaluation fundamentals 01

The aim of this chapter is to provide a conceptual framework for the process of job evaluation. It covers the following topics:

- definition;
- purpose;
- the meaning of value;
- features of job evaluation;
- the basis of job evaluation methodology.

A glossary of job evaluation terms is provided in Appendix A.

Job evaluation defined

Job evaluation is a systematic process for establishing the relative worth of jobs within an organization. The summary in Table 1.1 of what job evaluation is and what it is not was provided by ACAS (2014).

Purpose of job evaluation

Job evaluation aims to generate the information required to provide, in the words of Elliott Jaques (1961), 'equitable pay' by using fair, sound and consistent judgements to develop and maintain an internally equitable grade and pay structure. This means paying particular attention to the provision of equal pay for work of equal value.

Table 1.1   What job evaluation is and is not

Job evaluation is	Job evaluation is not
• Systematic	• Scientific
• Consistent	• An exact measurement of duties or tasks performed
• A good basis for a fair pay system	
• A way of getting a hierarchy of jobs on which to base a grading structure	• A way of judging a job holder's performance
	• A way of allocating pay rates

An alternative view was provided by Gupta and Jenkins (1991) who argued that the basic premise of job evaluation is that certain jobs 'contribute more to organizational effectiveness and success than others, are worth more than others and should be paid more than others'. This is all right as far as it goes but it neglects the need for internal equity or comparable worth.

The meaning of value

The *Concise Oxford Dictionary* defines value as 'worth' and worth as 'of value equivalent to'. Value, like beauty, can be said to be in the eye of the beholder. And it has a number of different meanings, namely the concepts of intrinsic value, relative value, the labour theory of value and market value.

Intrinsic value

The belief that jobs have intrinsic value that belongs naturally to them because of what they are has strongly influenced traditional job evaluation methods. This particularly applies to schemes in which the value of jobs is measured by scoring them, thus indicating that the worth or 'size' of a job is so many points. But job evaluation points have no meaning in themselves and therefore cannot be used in absolute terms to define the value of a job. The leading pragmatist John Dewey (1916) did not accept intrinsic value as an inherent or enduring property of things. Intrinsic value, he claimed, is always relative to a situation.

Relative value

The value of anything is always relative to the value of something else. It is this notion that governs the comparative nature of job evaluation which aims to establish the relative value (comparable worth) of jobs to one another so that internal equity can be achieved. The rates of pay for jobs within the organization are also compared with those outside the organization (market rate comparisons) so that pay levels can be competitive. A grade structure (a sequence or hierarchy of grades, bands or levels into which roles of comparable worth are placed) can signify that the roles grouped into one grade are of greater value than the grade below and of lower value than the grade above. But it can also define levels of responsibility in an organization, thus producing a career structure. A pay structure, which will be influenced by market comparisons, attaches financial values to roles and, where appropriate, pay ranges to grades.

Labour theory of value

The labour theory of value originated by Karl Marx (1867) treats labour as a commodity and states that the value of a product depends on the amount of labour required to produce it. Nielsen (2002) argues that 'job content'-based evaluation methodology, ie valuing jobs by reference to the duties carried out by job holders, is a Marxist approach and is no more relevant today than most of the other views expressed by Marx on political economy. This, he claimed, is because valuing jobs according to their content ignores market considerations.

Market value

The rate of pay for a job or a person is a price like any other price and rates in the external market (market rates) are affected by demand and supply considerations operating in what is likely to be an imperfect market. These affect rates of pay within organizations (the internal market) because they influence the ability of those organizations to attract and retain the sort of people they need. This is the argument used by Nielson (2002) to support market pricing:

Typical job evaluation systems set the prices of jobs by looking at factors that bear no relation to and are abstractions from the jobs themselves. Thus they abrogate the laws of supply and demand that set the prices of goods and services in the marketplace.

Implications

The meanings attached to value can be complementary (intrinsic value, labour theory) or contradictory (labour theory and market value, intrinsic and relative value). To a greater or lesser extent, they can all influence beliefs on what job evaluation is attempting to value and how to set about it. For example, belief in the prime significance of market value may lead to a focus on market pricing, belief in intrinsic value could lead to the use of traditional job content evaluation techniques, and belief in relative value might encourage the use of analytical matching (comparing jobs factor by factor) or market pricing. These beliefs are often subliminal but need to be articulated to achieve a satisfactory and understandable basis for valuing jobs.

Features of job evaluation

Job evaluation as described in this book involves comparisons and judgements about the value or worth of jobs. It is often stated that job evaluation is about jobs, not people. It is indeed not concerned with measuring the performance of people in their jobs but in today's more fluid organizations the work that people actually do is determined not just by a conventional idea of a 'job' but also by their own capability. It is people who create value, not jobs, and roles often evolve in accordance with the strengths and limitations of the people who fill them. Conventional job evaluation schemes may find it difficult to deal with this issue. And when it comes to paying individuals, organizations may feel that they have to take account of their 'market worth' – the value of the person in the marketplace – rather than where job evaluation has placed their job in a hierarchy.

In formal schemes, job evaluation aims to measure the value of jobs. Its other main features are that it is a measurement, comparative, judgemental, structured, and an analytical process.

Job evaluation as a measurement process

The assumption made by popular forms of job evaluation such as point-factor schemes and the Hay Guide Chart method is that it is possible to measure job value or worth. In job evaluation circles, reference is often made to the 'size' of jobs. But the ordinal (rank-ordered) numbers used in such schemes have no meaning in themselves and do not, because they cannot, represent any unit of measurement such as the number of items produced. It was noted by Emerson (1991) that, 'Ordinal structure without any ties to an empirical measuring system conveys the image of precision without providing any real, substantive measuring tool.' Points give an impression of accuracy but this is an illusion. The numerical scores are based on value judgements and do not produce mathematical certainty. It is perhaps preferable to regard job evaluation as a process for *comparing* job values. Some form of measurement in the form of points/scores may be used to assist in comparisons but these do not define value on their own.

Job evaluation as a comparative process

Job evaluation is fundamentally a comparative process. It deals with relationships, not absolutes. Jobs are compared with one another or with a scale (a graduated set of points as in a point-factor scheme or a defined hierarchy of job levels or grades as in a matching scheme or levelling). In some schemes, jobs are analysed into 'factors' (characteristics of the work involved, for example, skill, responsibility, complexity). These may be compared with a scale or with grade or job descriptions analysed under the same factor headings (analytical matching).

Job evaluation as a judgemental process

Job evaluation requires the exercise of judgement in interpreting data on jobs, comparing one job to another and comparing jobs against scales or factor by factor. It can be described as a subjective process carried out within an objective framework. Or as Graef Crystal (1971) memorably put it: 'Essentially, job evaluation boils down to organized rationalization.' Plachy (1987) commented: 'Job evaluation is not a scientific system; it is a human system. Human beings make mistakes. They lose their objectivity and consistency, no matter hard they try, no matter how great their integrity.'

Job evaluation as a structured process

A formal job evaluation scheme is structured in the sense that a framework is provided which aims to help evaluators make consistent and reasoned judgements. This framework consists of language and criteria used by all evaluators, although, because the criteria are always subject to interpretation, they do not guarantee that judgements will be either consistent or rational.

Job evaluation as an analytical process

Job evaluation is or should be based on a factual description of the characteristics of the jobs under consideration. This means that although judgemental, at least the judgements are informed. However, schemes may be described as analytical in the sense that jobs are analysed and compared in terms of defined factors, or non-analytical in the sense that 'whole jobs' which have not been analysed by factor are compared with one another. Properly designed and executed analytical schemes can help to ensure that judgements are structured and consistent.

The basis of job evaluation methodology

There are many different approaches to job evaluation – from the simple to the sophisticated. It can be conducted through a formal job evaluation scheme such as point-factor rating, matching or levelling that specifies systematic procedures for analysing jobs and criteria for assessing the value or worth of individual jobs and for comparing jobs with one another and placing them in a grade hierarchy. This is the meaning attached to the term 'formal job evaluation' in this book. Details of the different formal methods are given in Chapter 2. At the other extreme, jobs can be evaluated on an entirely informal basis as also described in Chapter 2.

Formal schemes can be used with varying degrees of informality just as an element of formality can be added to an informal approach. Different methods can be combined. Although formal job evaluation may work systematically it should not be treated as a rigid, monolithic and bureaucratic affair. It should instead be regarded as an approach, which may be applied flexibly. Process – how job evaluation is used – can be more important than the system itself when it comes to producing reliable, valid and acceptable results. This book often focuses on formal schemes but this does not mean that the importance of using them informally when appropriate is underestimated.

As defined in this book, formal job evaluation schemes such as point-factor rating, matching and levelling establish internal relativities – how the value or worth of jobs within an organization compare with one another. They do not directly determine rates of pay. However, they are associated with market pricing – the process of analysing market rates to establish external relativities in order to guide the development of a competitive pay structure, ie one in which levels of pay enable the organization to attract and retain the people it needs.

Market pricing

Market pricing can be used in the absence of a formal evaluation scheme to provide direct guidance on internal rates. This can be done systematically as an alternative to formal job evaluation and in effect this determines internal relativities. When market pricing is used like this it has been dubbed by Ellis et al (2004) as 'extreme market pricing'. This is not categorized in this book as a formal job evaluation scheme (one entirely concerned with internal relativities) although market pricing is treated as a formal job evaluation method in the United States. Market pricing techniques are examined in Chapter 10.

References

ACAS (2014) *Job Evaluation: Considerations and risk*, London, ACAS

Crystal, G (1970) *Financial Motivation for Executives*, New York, American Management Association

Dewey, J (1916) Objects of valuation, *Journal of Philosophy*, **15**, pp 9–35

Ellis, C M, Laymon, R G and LeBlanc, P V (2004) Improving pay productivity with strategic work valuation, *WorldatWork Journal*, Second Quarter, pp 56–68

Emerson, S M (1991) Job evaluation: a barrier to excellence, *Compensation & Benefits Review*, January–February, pp 4–17

Gupta, N and Jenkins, G D (1991) Practical problems in using job evaluation to determine compensation, *Human Resource Management Review*, **1** (2), pp 133–44

Jaques, E (1961) *Equitable Payment*, London, Heinemann

Marx, K (1867, translated in 1976) *Capital*, Harmondsworth, Penguin

Nielsen, N H (2002) Job content evaluation techniques based on Marxian economics, *WorldatWork Journal*, **11** (2), pp 52–62

Plachy, R J (1987) The point-factor job evaluation system: a step-by-step guide, part 2, *Compensation & Benefits Review*, September–October, pp 9–24

Job evaluation methodology 02

This chapter starts by describing formal approaches to job evaluation, listing the different kinds of analytical and non-analytical job evaluation schemes and the use of tailor-made, ready-made and hybrid schemes. Reference is also made to some of the off-the-shelf 'proprietary' schemes offered by management consultants. The use of non-formal methods of job evaluation is then discussed and the chapter ends with a description of computer-aided job evaluation.

Formal approaches to job evaluation

A formal approach to job evaluation involves the development and use of a structured scheme that provides for a systematic approach to be made to the two basic job evaluation activities, which are to:

1 establish the content of jobs through job analysis (see Chapter 6);

2 decide through an analytical or non-analytical system on the size of a job as represented by a points score, or the place of a job in a hierarchy of grades or levels, or the position of a job in a rank order.

The design and operation of a scheme usually involve the analysis and description of benchmark jobs – typical jobs that represent the different occupations and levels of work in an organization and can be used as points of reference when designing a scheme and with which other jobs can be compared and evaluated.

A scheme can be analytical or non-analytical.

Analytical job evaluation schemes

Analytical job evaluation schemes are based on a process of breaking whole jobs down into a number of defined factors. The advantages of an analytical approach are that first, evaluators have to consider each of the characteristics of the job separately before forming a conclusion about its relative value and second, they are provided with defined yardsticks or guidelines which help to increase the objectivity and consistency of judgements. It can also provide a defence against an equal pay claim.

In point-factor schemes jobs are analysed to establish the extent to which each factor is present and then scored by reference to a graduated scale of points attached to each factor in a set of factors. In analytical matching schemes jobs are allocated to grade profiles (job-to-grade matching) or compared to benchmark job profiles (job-to-job matching) analysed under the same factor headings by identifying the grade or job profile which most closely matches that of the job to be evaluated.

In the UK, point-factor rating and analytical matching as described in Chapters 7 and 8 are the most commonly used schemes. Analytical levelling schemes (levelling is analogous to job-to-grade matching – see Chapter 9) in which the levels of work in an organization are defined in terms of a number of factors, and jobs are slotted into those levels by reference to those factors, are becoming more popular. The other two less-used analytical methods are factor comparison and graduated factor comparison as described below.

Factor comparison

The original factor comparison method compared jobs factor by factor using a scale of money values to provide a direct indication of the rate for the job. It originated in the United States but was not adopted much in the UK. A revised version is available in the United States, and resembles a conventional point-factor scheme except that there are no level definitions. Jobs are ranked and placed on a scale for each factor. The points values for each factor according to the job's position are added to produce a total score.

Graduated factor comparison

Graduated factor comparison compares jobs factor by factor with a graduated scale. The scale may have only three value levels – for example lower, equal, higher – and no factor scores are used. This is a method often used by the independent experts engaged by Employment Tribunals to advise on an equal pay claim. Their job is simply to compare one job with one or two others, not to review internal relativities over the whole spectrum of jobs in order to produce a rank order. Independent experts may score their judgements of comparative levels, in which case graduated factor comparison resembles the point-factor method except that the number of levels and range of scores are limited, and the factors may not be weighted.

Graduated factor comparison can be used within organizations if there is a problem of comparable worth and no other analytical scheme is available. It can also be used in a benchmarking exercise to assess relativities across different categories of employees in the absence of a common analytical job evaluation scheme as long as the factors used are common to all the job categories under consideration.

Non-analytical job evaluation schemes

Non-analytical job evaluation schemes enable whole jobs to be compared in order to place them in a grade or a rank order – they are not analysed by reference to their elements or factors. A non-analytical scheme may stand alone or be used to help in the development of an analytical scheme. For example, the paired comparison technique described later can produce a rank order of jobs that can be used to test the outcomes of an evaluation using an analytical scheme. It is therefore helpful to know how non-analytical schemes function even if they are not used as the main technique.

Non-analytical schemes operate on a *job-to-grade* basis in which judgements are made by comparing a whole job with a defined hierarchy of job grades (non-analytical matching or job classification) – this involves matching a job description to a grade description. Alternatively, they may function on a *job-to-job* basis in which a job is compared with another job to decide whether it should be valued more, or less, or the same (ranking and 'internal benchmarking' processes).

Non-analytical schemes are relatively simple but rely on overall and potentially more subjective judgements than analytical schemes. Such judgements will not be guided by a factor plan and do not take account of the complexity of jobs. There is a danger therefore of leaping to conclusions about job values based on *a priori* assumptions which could be prejudiced. For this reason, non-analytical schemes do not provide a defence in a UK equal pay case.

There are four main types of non-analytical schemes: non-analytical matching or job classification, internal benchmarking, job ranking, and paired comparison (a statistical version of ranking). In addition, a levelling approach in which level definitions are not analysed into factors can be regarded as a non-analytical scheme.

Non-analytical matching (job classification)

This approach, traditionally referred to as job classification, is a job-to-grade procedure in which a 'whole' job description, ie one not analysed into factors, is compared with the grade definitions in a grade structure to establish the grade with which the job most closely corresponds. This process is known as matching or job slotting. The grade definitions may refer to such job characteristics as skill, decision making and responsibility but these are not treated separately as in analytical matching.

Internal benchmarking

Internal benchmarking is a job-to-job, non-analytical matching procedure in which the job under review is compared with any internal job which is believed to be properly graded and paid (an internal benchmark) and then placed into the same grade as that job. The comparison is made on a whole job basis without analysing the jobs factor by factor. This is what people often do intuitively when they are deciding on the value of jobs, although it is not usually dignified in job evaluation circles as a formal method of job evaluation. It can be classified as a formal method if there are specific procedures for preparing and setting out role profiles and for comparing profiles for the role to be evaluated with standard benchmark role profiles.

Job ranking

Whole-job ranking is the most primitive form of job evaluation. The process involves comparing whole jobs with one another and arranging them in order of their perceived value to the organization. In a sense, all evaluation schemes are ranking exercises because they place jobs in a hierarchy. The difference between simple ranking and analytical methods such as point-factor rating is that job ranking does not attempt to quantify judgements. Instead, whole jobs are compared – they are not broken down into factors or elements although, explicitly or implicitly, the comparison may be based on some generalized concept such as the level of responsibility. Job ranking or paired comparison ranking as described below is sometimes used as a check on the rank order obtained by point-factor rating.

Paired comparison ranking

Paired comparison ranking is a statistical technique that is used to provide a more sophisticated method of whole-job ranking. It is based on the assumption that it is always easier to compare one job with another than to consider a number of jobs and attempt to build up a rank order by multiple comparisons.

The technique requires the comparison of each job as a whole separately with every other job. If a job is considered to be of a higher value than the one with which it is being compared it receives two points; if it is thought to be equally important, it receives one point; if it is regarded as less important, no points are awarded. The scores are added for each job and a rank order is obtained.

Paired comparisons can be done factor by factor and in this case can be classified as analytical. A simplified example of a paired comparison ranking is shown in Table 2.1.

The advantage of paired comparison ranking over normal ranking is that it is easier to compare one job with another rather than having to make multiple comparisons. But it cannot overcome the fundamental objections to any form of whole-job ranking – that no defined standards for judging relative worth are provided, and it is not an acceptable method of assessing equal value or comparable worth. There is also a limit to the number of jobs that can be compared using this method – to evaluate 50 jobs requires 1,225 comparisons.

Table 2.1 A paired comparison

Job reference	A	B	C	D	E	F	Total score	Ranking
A	–	0	1	0	1	0	2	5=
B	2	–	2	2	2	0	8	2
C	1	0	–	1	1	0	3	4
D	2	0	1	–	2	0	5	3
E	1	0	1	0	–	0	2	5=
F	2	2	2	2	2	–	10	1

Paired comparisons are occasionally used analytically to compare jobs on a factor-by-factor basis.

Combined approaches

Organizations sometimes combine approaches and there are three ways of doing so:

1 *Point-factor rating/analytical matching* – point-factor rating or an analytical proprietary brand is used to evaluate benchmark posts as the basis for designing a grade structure in which grade profiles are defined analytically, and the remaining posts are graded by analytical matching. But a point-factor scheme can underpin a matching scheme by being invoked when a satisfactory match cannot be obtained. This is becoming a popular approach. It is used in the NHS, and the Hay Group job family modelling technique as used in a number of universities and elsewhere is often supported by their Guide Chart – Profile method of evaluation (in effect, a points scheme). As defined by Hay, a job family describes a number of different roles which are engaged in similar work and a job family model considers how many levels of that type of work there are and defines them in a way which clearly differentiates the levels. Jobs are evaluated by slotting them into the level in their job family that provides the closest match.

2 *Point-factor rating/non-analytical matching* – point-factor rating or an analytical proprietary brand is used to evaluate benchmark posts as the basis for designing a grade structure in which grades are defined non-analytically and the remaining posts are graded by slotting them into grades on a whole-job basis.

3 *Formal job evaluation/market rate comparison* – formal job evaluation is supplemented by information on market rates when developing pay structures, deciding on market supplements (additions to the base rate to reflect market rates) and fixing individual rates of pay.

The first two types of combination are used when it is believed that time will be saved by not extending benchmark point-factor rating to a large number of other posts.

Ready-made and tailor-made schemes

Job evaluation schemes can be developed entirely within an organization as described in Chapter 5. But it is common practice to buy them 'ready-made' or 'off-the-shelf' from a firm of management consultants – these are sometimes called a 'proprietary brand'. A number of consultancies offer such schemes. The Hay Group's Guide Chart-Profile method is the most widely used one. Other consultancies providing ready-made schemes include Aon Hewitt, Mercer, PricewaterhouseCoopers, SHL Group and Willis Towers Watson. Management consultants can also be engaged to help in the development of a tailor-made scheme in an organization, or they may modify (tailor) their standard scheme to suit the particular requirements of their clients.

Public sector schemes, often developed by consultancies, include:

- Agenda for Change job evaluation scheme (NHS);
- GLPC (Greater London Provincial Council);

- HERA (Higher Education Role Analysis);
- JEGS (Civil Service Job Evaluation and Grading Scheme);
- National Joint Council (NJC) for Local Government Services.

Informal approaches to job evaluation

Informal job evaluation does not use a structured approach. It depends on assumptions about relative internal value often based on matching one job with another in broad terms without always having the information provided by job descriptions for the job under consideration or for the job with which it is being compared. It is also likely to rely on market rate comparisons that may be crude generalizations formed from unreliable advertisements. The risk is that inequitable decisions will be made on the basis of subjective judgements that are not supported by any systematically assembled evidence.

There are, however, degrees of informality. A semi-formal approach might require some firm evidence to support a market pricing decision and the use of job descriptions to provide greater accuracy to the matching process through internal benchmarking.

Computer-aided job evaluation

Computer-aided job evaluation uses computer software to convert information about jobs into a job evaluation score or grade. It is generally underpinned by a conventional point-factor scheme. The 'proprietary brands' offered by consultants are often computer-aided. Computers may be used simply to maintain a database recording evaluations and their rationale. In the design stage they can provide guidance on weighting factors through multiple regression analysis, although this technique has been largely discredited and is little used now.

Methodology

The software used in a fully computer-aided scheme essentially replicates in digital form the thought processes followed by evaluators when conducting a 'manual' evaluation. It is based on defined evaluation decision rules built into the system shell. The software typically provides a facility for consistency checks by, for example, highlighting scoring differences between the job being evaluated and other benchmark jobs.

The two types of computer-aided evaluation are:

1 Schemes in which the job analysis data is either entered directly into the computer or transferred to it from a paper questionnaire. The computer software applies pre-determined rules to convert the data into scores for each factor and produce a total score. This is the most common approach.

2 Interactive computer-aided schemes in which the job holder and his or her manager sit in front of a PC and are presented with a series of logically interrelated questions, the answers to which lead to a score for each of the built-in factors in turn and a total score.

The case for computer-aided job evaluation

In a point-factor scheme that is not computer-aided, jobs are often evaluated by a panel that may include a broadly representative group of staff as well as line managers and one or more members of the HR department. The panel will have been trained in interpreting the factor plan and applying this in the evaluation of the job descriptions or questionnaires provided. It studies the job information and, by relating this to the factor level definitions and panel decisions on previous jobs, debates and agrees the level (and hence the score) that should be allocated for each factor. This is a well-understood process that has been tried and tested over more than 50 years and, properly applied, is generally accepted as a good approach by all concerned.

The problem with the panel approach is chiefly the way it is applied. The most common failings or disadvantages are:

- *Inconsistent judgements* – although the initial panel may be well trained, panel membership changes and, over time, the interpretation of the factor plan may also change. The presence or absence of a particularly strong-minded member may influence panel decisions.

- *Inadequate record of decisions* – each allocated factor level will, of necessity, be recorded but panels do not always conform to good practice by maintaining a record of how each decision was reached (a rationale). If an appeal is lodged, it can be difficult to assess whether or not the original panel took account of whatever evidence is presented in support of the appeal. The Gauge system of job evaluation helps to overcome this difficulty by recording the decision-making process.

- *Staff input required* – a panel of six or seven people (a typical size) may take an hour to evaluate each job if a traditional job-by-job approach is used. Up to 10 person hours could thus be spent evaluating each job. This is a substantial cost for any organization.

- *Time taken to complete the process* – assembling a quorum of trained panel members may take several weeks and, if their evaluations are subject to review by some higher-level review team (to minimize the risk of subsequent appeals) it can take two or three months to complete the whole process.

Incorporating computer-aided job evaluation as part of the process from the outset helps to overcome these problems. Depending on the type of scheme it can achieve greater consistency – the same input information gives the same output result. It can also increase the speed of evaluations, reduce the resources required and provide facilities for sorting, analysing, reporting on the input information and system outputs and record keeping (database).

However, it is worth remembering that the system can only support the job evaluation process by using the rules and algorithms that have been built into it. Human judgement is still required to design the scheme in the first place and to ensure that accurate job information is entered. In practice there is no such thing as 'computerized' job evaluation – only computer-aided evaluation.

The capabilities that can be found across a range of software packages are summarized in Table 2.2 below.

The software platforms have moved on considerably over recent years. Whereas initial computer-aided job evaluation schemes used to require the installation of a software package onto a stand-alone PC or server, most consultancy firms offering a computer-aided scheme

Table 2.2 Software job evaluation applications

Support to scheme design	
Development of weightings/scoring	Paired comparison to support development of weightings.
	Use of software package to develop weighting, eg SSPS for multiple regression analyses (often manipulated by consultant as part of development process – not part of client software package).
Data management	
Record keeping	Record of individual evaluation responses.
	Maintaining library of benchmark roles.
Data entry	Direct import of job questionnaires completed manually.
	Direct online responses to questionnaire by job holder or analyst; might be accompanied by guidance and the ability to refer to similar jobs (sometimes called an 'expert' system).
	Direct online responses that are tailored to responses already entered (an 'interactive' system).
Job descriptions/profiles	Ability to write job descriptions using a standard template, or evaluation responses generate a profile that is based on an adapted form of wording from the evaluation scheme.
Progress checking	System records status of all scores, eg provisional, final and multiple scores for same job where it is evaluated separately by more than one evaluator prior to evaluation team review.
Analysis and reporting	
Scoring	Calculation of evaluation scores using predetermined scoring/weighting – either built into standard package or agreed with client and built into software (usually on basis that client does not have access to the scoring model to make any changes).
	Sophisticated scoring capability including ability to build relationships between responses to separate questions.

(continued)

Table 2.2 (*Continued*)

Tailored reporting	Rank order listings either by total job score or factor by factor, either in order of calculated points score or by factor level entered (eg A, B, C etc).
	Analysis of evaluation results by function, gender or other pre-determined elements.
	Inter-site/division comparisons.
	Ability to generate customized reports.
Quality review	Quality checking of data entry for missing information.
	Identification of inconsistent scores, eg outside of pre-defined parameters, or unusual relativities between jobs (eg manager scores less than subordinate on decision making).

Additional applications linked to job evaluation

Pay modelling	Modelling grades salaries and costs of new pay structure (typically includes scattergrams, lines of best fit).
Equal pay review	Analysis by gender, disability, race or age for pay elements of total package, allowances and other benefits.
Competencies	Provides a link between job requirements and individual performance expectations and required behaviours.
Survey link	Direct link to consultants' pay database, based on evaluation points or bandings.

now provide for internet, intranet or PC access. The advantage of web-enabled systems is that the software is updated automatically, so there is no need to have to install the latest upgrade on-site.

A web-enabled or intranet system means that organizations can devolve the administration of their scheme around the organization, or where relevant, around the world. Where this is the case, the package will invariably provide for a range of security settings. This will typically allow for some locations or users to have read-only access, others will be able to enter and amend data for the jobs under their jurisdiction only, whereas at the highest level the system administrator will have complete access to all records in the system.

The case against computer-aided job evaluation

For some organizations the full approach is too expensive and elaborate a process for them to be bothered with. Others do not want to abandon the involvement of employees and their representatives in the traditional panel approach. There is also the problem of transparency in some applications. This is sometimes called 'the black box effect' – those concerned have difficulty in understanding the logic that converts the input information to a factor level score. Interactive systems such as those offered by Pilat Consultants (Gauge) aim to overcome this difficulty.

It is perhaps for these reasons that only 39 per cent of the respondents to the 2017 e-reward survey had computer-aided schemes although almost all of them used computers to maintain job evaluation records.

Use of schemes

The use of schemes by the respondents to the 2017 e-reward survey of job evaluation was as follows:

- point-factor rating – 68 per cent;
- levelling – 26 per cent;
- analytical job matching – 25 per cent;
- job classification –17 per cent;
- non-analytical job matching –10 per cent.

A number of respondents used more than one scheme, for example point-factor rating and analytical job matching.

References

Emerson, S M (1991) Job evaluation: a barrier to excellence, *Compensation & Benefits Review*, January–February, pp 4–17
e-reward (2017) *Job Evaluation Survey*, Stockport, e-reward
Plachy, R J (1987) The point-factor job evaluation scheme: a step by step guide, part 1, *Compensation & Benefits Review*, pp 9–24

Reviewing job evaluation 03

Job evaluation reviews are needed to establish the extent to which the arrangements are fit for purpose, ie how far they provide a clear, logical, fair and generally acceptable basis for developing and maintaining an equitable and competitive grade and pay structure that fits the organization's aims and context without imposing unacceptable costs or administrative burdens. The analysis should identify any specific problems and be followed by a diagnosis of the causes of the problems to indicate a course of action – to replace or revise the present approaches or to retain them. A choice can then be made of the approach to be adopted, as described in Chapter 4. This chapter covers the points to be considered with regard to the three main approaches – formal job evaluation, informal job evaluation and extreme market pricing. Consideration is also given to the objectives and specification of a formal scheme if that is required.

Formal job evaluation schemes

Formal job evaluation schemes can decay. The factors may no longer be appropriate, job descriptions can be inflated and scores may be manipulated, which can lead to inequities and 'grade drift' (unjustifiable upgradings). Schemes can be bureaucratic, time-consuming and expensive to operate. The checklist in Table 3.1 contains questions relating to these and other typical problems that can arise in established job evaluation schemes, especially if they have been functioning for some time.

Table 3.1   Checklist for reviewing the effectiveness of a formal job evaluation scheme

1	Does the scheme show any general signs of decaying?
2	In an analytical scheme, are the factors still appropriate in the light of changes in roles and the way in which work is organized, or new approaches to defining the core values and competencies of the organization?
3	In a points scheme, is there any evidence of 'point grabbing', ie using inflated role profiles or job descriptions to acquire the extra points needed to achieve an upgrading?
4	Does the scheme lead to or fail to control grade drift?
5	Are the results obtained by the scheme consistent, ie similar roles are valued the same in different functions or over time?
6	Has operating the scheme become a 'cottage industry', ie a time-consuming paper production process which creates unnecessary work and not added value?
7	Do employees understand how the scheme operates and how it influences grade and pay decisions?
8	Are employees and their representatives cynical about the scheme or openly hostile to it because they feel it functions unfairly or inconsistently?
9	Does the scheme provide a satisfactory basis for maintaining an equitable grade and pay structure?
10	Will the scheme provide an adequate defence in an equal pay case?

Table 3.2   Checklist for reviewing the effectiveness of an informal approach

1	Do we believe that relying on managerial judgement on internal and external relativities to determine rates of pay produces results that satisfy both management and employees?
2	Are we confident that we have got internal relativities right?
3	Do our methods of tracking and responding to information on market rates produce a competitive pay structure as indicated by our ability to attract and retain good-quality people?
4	Have we got the right information to develop and maintain an equitable grade and pay structure?
5	Are we vulnerable to an equal pay claim?

Informal approach

If an informal approach exists, the checklist in Table 3.2 can be used to review its effectiveness.

Extreme market pricing

The effectiveness of extreme market pricing, ie relying entirely on market rate data to determine competitive rates of pay and, in effect, internal relativities, depends largely on the validity of the data. Questions need also to be asked about how it impacts on internal equity. A checklist is set out in Table 3.3.

Decide whether to retain, modify or replace

The answers to these checklists will provide guidance on whether the formal scheme, the informal approach or reliance on market pricing

Table 3.3 Checklist for reviewing the effectiveness of extreme market pricing

1	Does the process ensure that pay levels are competitive?
2	Are the sources of information about market rates valid and reliable?
3	Has a good sample of benchmark roles been used for external comparisons?
4	Have good external matches been obtained for those benchmark roles?
5	Is the approach used to price roles for which external data is not available satisfactory?
6	Has the data been interpreted properly to allow for variations in information from different sources?
7	Does the use of market pricing result in any significant internal inequities?
8	Does the use of extreme market pricing leave us vulnerable to a successful equal pay claim?
9	Do managers and employees understand how market pricing works?
10	Do they accept the results as fair and equitable?

should be retained with, possibly, some modifications, or whether it needs to be replaced.

Retain, possibly with modification

The analysis of the present arrangements may indicate that they are perfectly satisfactory, but there will be few situations in which no improvements can be made, at least to the process of operation if not the approach itself.

Improving a formal job evaluation scheme

Improvements to a formal job evaluation scheme can be made by giving more guidance and training to managers and evaluators, monitoring the inputs to job evaluation (role profiles) and outcome of evaluations more carefully, exercising closer control over upgradings following job evaluations, streamlining job evaluation procedures, spending time on communicating how the scheme works, using analytical matching as the main process for evaluating roles (relegating the basic point-factor scheme to a support role), or making minor amendments to the factor plan (replacing a considerable part of it would constitute a new scheme).

It may also be decided that introducing a computer-aided system would diminish administrative burdens and provide for more consistency in judgements of value.

Possible improvements to an informal approach

Improving an informal approach probably means adding a degree of formality to decision making. Arrangements can be made for internal comparisons to be made by comparing specially prepared role profiles for the role under consideration with role profiles for benchmark roles – this could be described as internal benchmarking. External comparisons with market rates can be based on a more systematic review of data – going beyond reference to advertisements to scanning published survey material. These actions would mean in effect that a semi-formal approach has been adopted.

Improving extreme market pricing

Possible improvements to extreme market pricing include:

- ensuring that a representative sample of jobs is used to benchmark against external comparisons;

- reviewing existing and potential sources of market data to ensure that it is valid and reliable (see also Chapter 10);

- reviewing methods of interpreting and presenting data so that it gives clear guidance on any actions necessary;

- reviewing methods of pricing non-benchmark jobs for which no market data is available.

Replace present approach

It may be decided that tinkering with the present arrangements will do little good and the approach should be replaced. The choice will be between replacing an existing formal job evaluation scheme with a new scheme, moving from formal job evaluation to market pricing or vice versa, or changing from formal arrangements to informal ones or vice versa. The factors affecting this choice will be the organization's context, including its values, size and complexity, the national or international nature of its operations, and the degree to which it is competing for high-quality people. These are discussed in Chapter 4.

If it is also believed that a revised grade structure is required, for example reducing the number of grades, this is a further argument for introducing a new scheme. But this decision should not be taken lightly. New schemes can take a lot of time, trouble and money to develop and install and can cause disruption and dissatisfaction.

Points for consideration – formal job evaluation

A checklist of the points to be considered when deciding whether to retain or introduce formal job evaluation is given in Table 3.4.

Table 3.4   Checklist of points to be considered when deciding whether to introduce a formal job evaluation scheme

Do we need formal job evaluation for any of the following reasons?
1   The present approach results in inequitable rates of pay.
2   A grade structure is required which is based on a systematic, logical and fair process of determining relativities.
3   A sounder and more defensible method of grading jobs is required.
4   Without it we are vulnerable to an expensive equal pay claim.
5   It is required to inform equal pay reviews.
6   Employees or their representatives are pressing for a fairer and more transparent method of making grade and pay decisions.

Points for consideration – extreme market pricing

The questions affecting the choice of extreme market pricing are simply:

1 Is our main concern the need to be competitive in the job marketplace?

2 Do we believe that formal job evaluation schemes are a waste of time and money?

3 Are we certain that we can get good market rate data?

4 Do we believe that market pricing will produce an internally equitable pay structure?

5 Do we care whether pay is internally equitable or not?

Question 5 may not be posed as crudely as this, but a negative answer, even if not stated explicitly, may underpin the decision to go for market pricing. It may be felt that such an answer is deplorable in terms of achieving equal pay for work of equal value within the organization, but it represents the approach adopted by many businesses that use market pricing.

Points for consideration – informal approach

The questions to be answered when reviewing how well an informal approach suits the organization's needs are:

1 Are we satisfied that we can price jobs without a formal scheme?

2 Do we believe that our informal approach will enable us to offer competitive rates of pay?

3 Does our informal approach create internal inequities and would it matter if it did?

Define objectives

If it is decided that a new or revised formal approach is required, it is necessary to be clear about what is to be achieved from the new scheme before producing a specification of requirements.

A guide to the possible objectives that might be set was provided by the respondents to the 2017 e-reward survey of job evaluation. The most common objectives in order of popularity were:

- help manage internal job relativities;
- provide basis for design and maintenance of rational and defensible pay structure;
- compare internal pay levels with market rates;
- ensure equitable pay structure;
- ensure the principle of equal pay for work of equal value;
- assimilate newly-created or changing jobs into existing structures;
- harmonize pay structures as a result of merger or acquisition;
- facilitate lateral career moves and internal mobility.

Other objectives not mentioned by the respondents were to provide a basis for career planning or to enable the better analysis of the organization's structure by levelling, ie defining levels of responsibility and how roles fit into them.

Specification

A specification for a formal job evaluation scheme provides the basis for evaluating the different approaches and for briefing consultants.

Table 3.5 Example of job evaluation scheme specification

The job evaluation scheme should:	
1	Overcome the problems of the present arrangements, namely inappropriate factor plan and inability to control grade drift.
2	Provide the information needed to develop a new pay structure with fewer grades.
3	Be analytical.
4	Be based on a factor plan aligned as far as possible with the competency framework.
5	Be computerized to minimize the time and resources used to administer it.
6	Be acceptable to the trade unions.

It flows from the objectives and has to fit the circumstances and culture of the organization. The specification should set out what the scheme is intended to achieve, the type of scheme required (eg analytical), whether it should be a computer-aided system, and any concerns of management, staff or trade unions that may affect it. An example of a specification drawn up for a large local authority is given in Table 3.5.

Reference

e-reward (2017) *Job Evaluation Survey*, Stockport, e-reward

Choice of approach

There is plenty of choice when it comes to deciding what to do about job evaluation after the present arrangements have been reviewed as described in Chapter 3. The first choice is whether to go in for extreme market pricing rather than some form of job evaluation. Assuming that extreme market pricing is not wanted, another choice is whether to use formal or informal methods of valuing jobs. If formal methods are preferred, the choice is between one of the various approaches available.

Extreme market pricing?

Extreme market pricing is the preferred approach to valuing jobs when it is believed that 'the market rules OK' and that what really matters is to pay competitive rates based on establishing what jobs are worth in the marketplace. Another common reason for adopting extreme market pricing is the belief that it obviates the need for spurious, expensive, bureaucratic and time-wasting job evaluation schemes.

Supporters of extreme market pricing are not very concerned about internal equity. They claim that market rates are ascertainable facts not subject to the judgements present in traditional approaches. But they fail to recognize that market pricing is equally judgemental because of the difficulty of matching external jobs with internal ones. The accuracy of market pricing depends on the availability of robust market data and the quality of the job-matching process, ie comparing like with like.

Formal or informal?

A formal approach involves the use of a job evaluation scheme while an informal one means that jobs are priced on the basis of largely unsupported assumptions about what they are worth. This may not be a conscious decision. A company can use informal methods (or no methods) simply because that's what it has always done and because it never occurs to its management that there is an alternative. But it may decide deliberately that informality fits its circumstances best. The factors that affect the choice of approach are explained below.

Objectives

The objectives of job evaluation include deciding on the level or grade of jobs, developing and maintaining grade and pay structures, providing a framework for career planning, contributing to organizational analysis and design, achieving equal pay for work of equal value, and creating a defence against equal pay claims. These objectives are more likely to be achieved in larger organizations if a formal job evaluation scheme is used or if a formal and systematic approach to extreme market pricing is adopted.

The type, size and complexity of the organization

The public and voluntary sectors are more likely to use formal job evaluation. The survey conducted by e-reward in 2017 established that all the public-sector organizations and 92 per cent of the voluntary sector organizations had a job evaluation scheme. The proportion of private-sector businesses with a scheme was 70 per cent.

Smaller and start-up organizations are less likely to use formal job evaluation than large, complex and established ones. A small or a new business may believe – rightly or wrongly – that it does not need the support of an elaborate job evaluation scheme to run its pay system.

Organization culture

The core values of organizations will affect their attitude to job evaluation. Those that believe strongly in equity, fairness and transparency may be more inclined to use a formal scheme and, while sensitive to market rates, will not allow their pay system to be driven by them. Organizations whose values are dominated by the need to achieve competitive advantage and enhance shareholder value may be less inclined to give prominence to the ideal of internal equity and are more likely to go in for an informal approach extreme market pricing.

Work and organization structure

Job evaluation is more likely to be used formally where the work is relatively structured, prescribed or routine, as in public and private bureaucracies and manufacturing. It is less likely to occur in organizations largely staffed by knowledge workers (eg research and development) or creative workers (eg advertising agencies).

International firms

International firms have a variety of practices depending on their structure and management processes. Some may prefer to use a formal system to ensure a degree of uniformity in dealing with grade and pay issues, for example the pay of local staff, expatriates and third-country nationals in their international units or subsidiaries. They may also be interested in job evaluation as a means of developing international career pathways.

The approach adopted may be a traditional formal scheme coupled with market pricing through local pay surveys. Some international organizations use the services of management consultants to establish rates of pay in different countries using a common structure of grade levels.

The external environment

The choice will be influenced by the labour market – if it is highly competitive, extreme market pricing is more likely to be favoured. It will also be affected by equal pay legislation and, sometimes, the views of the national trade unions.

Summary

A formal approach is more likely:

- in larger, more complex, more bureaucratic organizations;
- when there are strong values in favour of equity, fairness and transparency in the organization;
- when it is believed that equal pay considerations are important.

An informal approach is more likely:

- in small and start-up organizations;
- when it is believed that formal job evaluation is unnecessary, costly, cumbersome or bureaucratic;
- when it is considered that the market is all-important.

What type of formal job evaluation scheme?

If it is decided not to use extreme market pricing and that a formal rather than informal approach is appropriate, a choice has to be made between the various formal approaches. The criteria for choice are set out below. In the light of these criteria, consideration has to be given to whether to choose a 'ready-made' scheme as offered by management consultants or other suppliers, or whether a 'tailor-made' scheme designed specifically for the organization is preferable. Another possibility is to have a 'hybrid' scheme, one based on a ready-made scheme but adapted to suit the organization. It is also necessary to consider whether the scheme should be analytical or non-analytical and in either case what type of scheme is best.

Criteria

The main criteria for selecting a formal scheme are that it should be:

- thorough in analysis and capable of impartial application;
- applicable to all the jobs in the organization, and if factors are used, they should be common to all those jobs;

- reasonably easy to administrate – the scheme should not be too complex, costly or time-consuming to design, implement or maintain;

- transparent – the processes used in the scheme, from the initial job analysis through to the grading decision, should be clear to all concerned;

- non-discriminatory – the scheme should meet equal pay for work of equal value requirements.

Choice between a tailor-made, ready-made or hybrid scheme

A choice is required between a specially designed tailor-made scheme, a 'ready-made' consultant's scheme (a 'proprietary brand'), or a 'hybrid' scheme (a modified consultant's scheme). The advantages and disadvantages of each approach are summarized in Table 4.1.

Analytical or non-analytical?

A comparison of the features, advantages and disadvantages of analytical and non-analytical approaches is given in Table 4.2.

What type of formal scheme?

A comparison of the various schemes and their advantages and disadvantages is shown in Table 4.3.

The choice of scheme should be made by weighing up the advantages and disadvantages and assessing the extent to which the alternatives meet the criteria.

Reference

e-reward (2017) *Job Evaluation Survey*, Stockport, e-reward

Table 4.1 Choice between a tailor-made, ready-made or hybrid scheme

Choice	Advantages	Disadvantages
Ready-made A consultant's 'proprietary' brand	• Tried and tested, with an established reputation • The consultants can draw on extensive experience of implementing similar schemes • Does not require intensive design effort • May link to pay database • Computer support may be available as part of the package • Consultancy may have international network and database	• Factors may not suit the requirements, characteristics and culture of the organization • May not lead to high level of internal ownership • May be difficult to explain rationale for scoring and weighting • Can lead to ongoing reliance on external provider • May include elements or supporting processes that do not meet organizational requirements, eg lengthy job descriptions • May be costly
Tailor-made A scheme specially designed for the organization	• Reflects the values and language of the organization – focuses on what is important • Fits the particular needs at the time • Participative design process likely to lead to greater buy-in • No ongoing reliance on external provider • Can be aligned to competency framework	• Needs investment of considerable time and resources to develop scheme • Unless expertise is available in-house, needs external support to develop
Hybrid A proprietary scheme modified to a degree (eg amended factor plan) to fit the organization's particular needs	• Enables the proprietary scheme to be customized to a degree • Draws on external experience, so saves on design time • Gives a starting point to the design process, but gives opportunities to engage employees	• Needs careful design input and implementation to avoid same risks as for proprietary scheme • Need to avoid 'cherry picking' factors or scheme design elements that do not logically hang together

Table 4.2 Comparison of analytical and non-analytical approaches to job evaluation

Approach	Features	Types	Advantages	Disadvantages
Analytical	Decisions are made about the relative value or size of jobs by reference to an analysis of the level at which various defined factors or elements are present in a job. The set of factors used in a scheme is called the *factor plan*. This defines each of the factors used (these should be present in all the jobs to be evaluated), the levels within each factor and, in point-factor schemes, the scores available at each level.	• Point-factor • Analytical matching • Combined • Analytical levelling	• Systematic • Provide evaluators with defined yardsticks which help to increase the objectivity and consistency of judgements • Provide a defence against an equal pay claim	• Can be expensive and time-consuming to design or implement • Can be over-complex • Do not ensure either complete objectivity or consistency
Non-analytical	Whole jobs are compared to place them in a grade or a rank order – they are not analysed by reference to their elements or factors.	• Non-analytical matching (job classification) • Non-analytical levelling • Job ranking	• Can be developed quite easily • Provide a simple and quick method of grading jobs or establishing relativities (rank orders)	• Rely on overall and potentially subjective judgements which may be insufficiently guided by a factor plan and do not take account of the complexity of jobs • No defined standards for judging relative worth are provided • Do not provide a defence in an equal pay case

Table 4.3 Comparison of formal job evaluation schemes

Scheme	Characteristics	Advantages	Disadvantages
Point-factor rating	An analytical approach in which separate factors are scored and added together to produce a total score for the job which can be used for comparison and grading purposes.	As long they are based on proper job analysis, point-factor schemes provide evaluators with defined yardsticks, which help to increase the objectivity and consistency of judgements and reduce the over-simplified judgement made in non-analytical job evaluation. They provide a defence against equal value claims as long as they are not in themselves discriminatory.	Can be complex and give a spurious impression of scientific accuracy – judgement is still needed in scoring jobs. Not easy to amend the scheme as circumstances, priorities or values change.
Analytical matching	Grade profiles are produced which define the characteristics of jobs in each grade in a grade structure in terms of a selection of defined factors. Role profiles are produced for the jobs to be evaluated set out on the basis of analysis under the same factor headings as the grade profiles. Role profiles are 'matched' with the range of grade profiles to establish the best fit and thus grade the job.	If the matching process is truly analytical and carried out with great care, this approach saves time by enabling the evaluation of a large number of jobs, especially generic ones, to be conducted quickly and in a way which should satisfy equal value requirements.	The matching process could be more superficial and therefore suspect than evaluation through a point-factor scheme. In the latter approach there are factor-level definitions to guide judgements and the resulting scores provide a basis for ranking and grade design which is not the case with analytical matching. Although matching on this basis may be claimed to be analytical, it might be difficult to prove this in an equal value case.

Non-analytical matching (job classification)	Grades are defined in a structure in terms of the level of responsibilities involved in a hierarchy. Jobs are allocated to grades by matching the job description with the grade description (job slotting).	Simple to operate; standards of judgement when making comparisons are provided in the shape of the grade definitions.	Can be difficult to fit complex jobs into a grade without using over-elaborate grade definitions; the definitions tend to be so generalized that they are not much help in evaluating borderline cases or making comparisons between individual jobs; does not provide a defence in an equal value case.
Combined point-factor/ matching approach	Point-factor rating is used to evaluate benchmark posts and design the grade structure and the remaining posts are graded by analytical or non-analytical matching.	Combines the advantages of both methods.	Can be more complex to explain and administer. If non-analytical matching (job classification) is used rather than analytical matching the disadvantages set out above apply so there may be more of a need to revert to the full point-factor scheme in the event of disagreement.
Levelling	Levels of work in an organization are defined and described in terms of decision-making accountabilities and jobs are fitted into those levels.	Concerned with the design of an organization, how work is structured in a hierarchy and the career paths available. It aims to fuse job evaluation with OD and talent management considerations. This can extend its purpose well beyond that of a traditional job evaluation programme.	As for analytical and non-analytical matching.

Developing job evaluation 05

In this chapter the approach to developing a tailor-made job evaluation scheme is examined. The chapter includes descriptions of the overall development programme and its two main stages – design and implementation.

The development programme

The development programme for a point-factor scheme involves selecting and analysing benchmark jobs (job analysis is covered in Chapter 6), creating a factor plan and testing the factor plan on those jobs. This leads to the development of a grade structure. A matching scheme involves designing a grade or level structure, defining the grades and testing the process of allocating benchmark posts to them.

Following the initial design stages a survey of market rates usually takes place to inform the design of a pay structure. This typically consists of pay ranges added to the grade structure.

The implementation stage in a development programme involves evaluating and grading all the jobs not dealt with as benchmarks in the design stage, allocating those jobs to grades, assimilating employees into the new or revised pay structure, dealing with the protection of employees from any reduction in their earnings because they are paid more than the maximum of their new pay grade, and hearing appeals against grading.

Stages

The stages in a development programme are described below.

1. Pre-planning

Decisions are made on the need for a new scheme or to revise an existing one; objectives are defined; the type of scheme is selected; consideration is given to who should be involved in developing the scheme and whether outside help in the shape of consultants is required; and a project plan is produced covering both design and implementation.

The costs are calculated and budgeted for. These include the cost of buying in external support and software, if needed. Importantly, they also include the costs of assimilating employees to a new pay grade after the scheme has been implemented. Assimilation policies usually provide for those paid above their new pay grade to be 'red-circled' which, as provided for in a typical protection policy, means that their pay is protected at its present level, although the protection period may be limited. At the same time those paid below their new pay grade are 'green-circled', which means that their pay is increased to at least the minimum of their new pay grade immediately or, if the increase is considerable, say more than 10 per cent, over a period of two or three years. Thus there is almost inevitably an increase in payroll costs and this can typically amount to 2 or 3 per cent. It should also be recognized that in addition to the direct financial costs there is the cost of the time taken by people in the organization for designing and operating the scheme (opportunity cost).

The following principles should be taken into account when considering the design programme:

- The scheme should be based on a thorough analysis of the jobs to be covered and the types of demands made on those jobs to determine what factors or level definitions are appropriate in the context of the organization's working environment and culture.

- The scheme should facilitate impartial judgements of relative job values.

- Factors or the grade/level elements in a matching scheme should cover the whole range of jobs to be evaluated without favouring any particular type of job or occupation and without discriminating on the grounds of gender, race, disability or for any other reason – the scheme should fairly measure features of female-dominated jobs as well as male-dominated jobs.

- Through the use of common evaluation criteria and methods of analysis and evaluation, the scheme should enable benchmarking to take place of the relativities between jobs in different functions or job families.
- The scheme should be simple to operate.
- The scheme should be transparent; everyone concerned should know how it works – the basis upon which the evaluations are produced.
- Special care should be taken in developing a grade structure to ensure that grade boundaries are placed appropriately and that the allocation of jobs to grades is not discriminatory.
- Plenty of time should be allowed.

2. Resource the project

An early decision needs to be made on what resources will be required to complete a job evaluation project. It is wise not to underestimate this. The internal resources required will be someone to direct and control the project (often an HR or reward specialist), job analysts, project administrators, communication specialists and project team members. The job analysts will need to be trained in the techniques they will use.

3. Set up project team

A project team is set up, consisting of managers, employee or union representatives and HR or reward specialists who will be involved in the design of the scheme. A team may be chaired or facilitated by a senior manager or an HR/reward specialist. An outside consultant who has been engaged to advise on the scheme's development sometimes carries out this role.

4. Produce project plan

Project planning means identifying and defining the activities required, ensuring that the resources required are available, estimating times for completing each stage of the project and drawing up and maintaining a project timetable. The principles to follow in drawing up a project plan are:

- Allow plenty of time – it is likely to take longer than you think.

- Identify the key stages in the projects – the events that have to take place and the activities required to make those events happen.

- Clarify any interdependencies between stages.

- Define the criteria to be used to assess whether satisfactory progress has been made.

- Identify the key decisions to be made.

- Identify the responsibilities for managing the project, conducting each stage, monitoring and reporting on progress, reviewing progress and making decisions.

- Remember when planning the project that a frequent major cause for delay is getting decisions agreed by steering groups or higher authorities.

- Build communications into the project plan from the outset. Job evaluation implementation starts at project inception, as early communications set the scene for how credible the scheme will ultimately be. It is often helpful to have a separate communications plan that runs alongside the technical development plan.

- Develop project control systems. Take account of organizational style and culture in developing the plan. Try and make a realistic assessment of how many drafts of the scheme will be needed before it is signed off. Is the organization highly analytical? How feasible is it to drive decisions through the steering group or senior management team, and to what extent are they likely to want to see a number of iterations/drafts at each stage? Build in contingency time, as appropriate.

- Allow time for testing the scheme.

5. Design scheme

A draft scheme is produced. Descriptions of how the two most popular types of formal job evaluation schemes – point-factor and matching – are designed are given in Chapters 7 and 8 respectively.

6. Decide on job evaluation procedures and policies

The procedures for operating the job evaluation scheme and the policies and procedures for appeals, assimilation and protection (see the last section of this chapter) are drawn up and agreed. It is advisable to do this at a fairly early stage in the programme, especially if they have to be negotiated with trade unions.

7. Analyse and evaluate benchmark jobs

Benchmark jobs are selected and analysed in accordance with any factor plan that has been incorporated in the design of either a point-factor or job-to-job matching scheme. A point-factor scheme will require the panel to:

- study the job description or role profile;
- establish for each factor in the scheme the level at which it is present by comparing the information available on that aspect of the job with the level definitions in the factor plan;
- decide which provides the best fit (often a judgemental process);
- agree scores for each factor according to its level;
- add the factor scores to produce a total score;
- record a rationale for their decision.

Analytical matching requires the matching panel to study a role profile analysed in terms of pre-defined evaluation elements and match this to a similarly analysed level profile or benchmark role profile using pre-determined matching rules or 'protocols'.

It is advisable to test the draft scheme on benchmark jobs. There is typically at least one iteration before an acceptable scheme is produced.

8. Create grade and pay structure

At this stage of designing a point-factor or matching scheme, the outcome of the benchmark evaluations and an examination of the job/organization structure form the basis for a decision on the grade structure. Grades are defined in terms of job evaluation points or grade descriptors (profiles) as described in Chapter 11. In a levelling scheme (see Chapter 9) the level structure will be determined on the basis of organizational analysis and defined in terms of predetermined criteria. A survey of market rates is conducted and the grade structure extended into a grade and pay structure.

9. Evaluate remaining jobs

The remaining non-benchmark jobs are evaluated and slotted into the grade or level structure. As described earlier, with a point-factor scheme this can be a lengthy and tedious process. This is why matching is increasingly used at this stage as it is much less time-consuming. An underpinning point-factor scheme may only be deployed when it has been impossible to obtain a good match.

10. Assimilate employees into the new or revised structure

Individual employees are assimilated into the grade and pay structure and an analysis is made of the number of individuals who will have either to be red- or green-circled.

The cost of increasing the pay of employees to bring them into their new pay grade is calculated and if it is more than the amount budgeted it may be necessary to redesign the grade and pay structure so that after assimilation, the pay of a greater number of employees is within their new grade.

11. Inform individual employees

Individual employees are informed about their new pay grade and, where necessary, the arrangements for protecting their pay.

12. Hear appeals

Appeals by employees against their grading are heard in accordance with the appeal procedure.

Communicating to employees

An important activity at all stages of a development programme is the communication to employees of the aims of job evaluation, how it works and how they will be affected by it. A job evaluation programme creates interest and concern amongst all employees. There will be expectations and fears that may or may not be reasonable. In some cases staff may believe that they will get more money. In others there may be concerns that the process is being used to review cost-cutting/restructuring opportunities. In practice, there are usually some winners (staff whose pay is below the minimum for their new grade who will therefore get an increase) and some losers (staff whose pay is above the maximum for their new grade and, although protected against any immediate reduction, may eventually 'mark time' or even lose pay when they revert to the rate for their grade at the end of the protection period). The pay of the majority of people will be unchanged. In contrast, trade unions have sometimes claimed that the aim of management is to use job evaluation to reduce pay all round.

There are key stages in a job evaluation development project when communication is essential: as the project starts, before employees are involved in job analysis, during the design stage, when the scheme design is complete and before and during the implementation programme. Regular progress bulletins should be issued.

It is essential to reinforce the basic messages regularly; for example, the purpose of the project and how people will be affected (eg no one should expect to gain but no one will lose at the time when the scheme is implemented).

Practical guidance

The advice of the practitioners who responded to the 2017 e-reward job evaluation survey on designing and introducing a job evaluation (JE) scheme is set out below in the form of dos and don'ts.

Design practice

Do:

- Clearly think about the purpose and rationale for introducing JE and how it will be used across various HR processes.

- Ensure you have a clear objective for the scheme.

- Keep it simple and transparent.

- Apply one scheme for all jobs in the organization. Make sure the scheme is a good fit for the types of roles in your organization. Keep good records to track outcomes for reference and consistency. Invest time in ensuring consistency and quality of job description information before starting the evaluation process. Have a central resource that is accountable for the scheme and ensure that peer review is built into the process.

- Create materials that describe the different levels in a way that's meaningful for your business (eg don't necessarily just use the standard off-the-shelf descriptors).

- Build in language and elements the business understands.

- Consider what you want to be important when weighting factors. Ask people's opinion of what the important and less important factors are. Ensure the factors cover all aspects of all jobs in the organization. Trial the draft scheme to see if it works.

- Consult widely with your senior leaders.

- Consult, educate, promote, be transparent.

- Decide on the overall number of grades in your internal grading structure – these could span multiple (Hay Group or similar) levels, especially at the higher grades to maintain flexibility.

- Extensively test your design by doing some benchmark evaluations and thoroughly moderate the outcomes. Get your job description/ job profile template right and make sure managers are clear about what they are for and how best they can be completed. Thoroughly train and prepare your job analysts – a consistent approach and application is key to ensuring good-quality outputs – and quality check them until you're comfortable they're doing it right.

- Have a clear understanding of differentials between one grade and another.

- Put together a project team with clear roles and responsibilities and project timeline; put aside time to plan for communication strategy and engagement with key stakeholders; do thorough research of different JE approaches to see what would fit the best within your organization; be clear what benefits JE will bring to your organization in terms of retention, recruitment, financial impact etc; schedule position review interviews with team managers; at an early stage of the process (or even before embarking on the project) make sure that you have a database of all job descriptions and that they are up to date. Involve unions/staff representatives by keeping them informed on the project progress.

- Use a recognized scheme (eg Hay) but look at tailoring as one size does not fit all.

- Remember that with all evaluation systems more or less 90 per cent of the roles are levelled without any discussion. The last and tricky 10 per cent are hard no matter which approach you take. Do not design a system simply to defend levelling results for the last 10 per cent. Keep it simple and leave room for manoeuvring. Reduce complexity. Make it understandable. Use the time that you save on complex evaluation methods to discuss the scheme and its implications with management.

Don't:

- Assume there is a perfect solution.

- Add layers of complexity in an effort to be able to explain/justify matching; the outcome will be a system that is inoperable.

- Design a process for now – think ahead to where the organization may be in one to five years.

- Expect most managers to be competent or capable of writing good-quality job descriptions and accountability statements.

- Get too detailed in your descriptions/factors as this will only take away flexibility and lead to endless discussions... but don't leave it too general either.

- Make it cumbersome to maintain or unnecessarily bureaucratic.
- Over-engineer the process, which could lead to a cottage industry of role evaluations.
- Rush the process – there may be a lot of tweaking or going back to the drawing board.
- Rely on existing job descriptions that are unlikely to be fit for purpose.
- Underestimate the time the project and design stage will take.
- Use a too large a panel of evaluators – six is a good number; more than this tends to become difficult to manage and gain consensus.

Introducing job evaluation

Do:

- Allow enough time for communication, create task force groups, ensure full understanding of the principles by the organization.
- Be open and transparent and communicate thoroughly with staff and unions.
- Be able to describe the scheme in simple terms all can understand.
- Communicate, communicate, communicate (all ways) – understanding by, and sensitivity to all is essential.
- Provide as much information to staff as possible to inform them of the process and reason for JE and to enable them to provide realistic and agreed information about their job for evaluation purposes.
- Decide on level of transparency of grading structures and how these read across to internal pay ranges. Separate the communication of new grades from any related to base pay changes as the latter is a more emotive subject.
- Ensure training of all HR personnel involved in the process and provide them with materials to engage their stakeholders. Be clear that the result needs to be 'felt fair' – there is never a perfect scientific answer.
- Ensure you have a buy-in from the senior management team; allow extra time for internal approvals, developing and implementing scheme governance before going live.

- Introduce in the context of other HR processes rather than just 'you were a grade x; now you are a band y'.
- Test in a live 'pilot' environment.

Don't:

- Think that it will be a perfect solution.
- Allow a 'cottage industry' culture to develop in respect of rewriting and re-evaluating roles.
- Allow too many exceptions – manage through pay protection red-circling rather than allowing grade drift before you start.
- Assume that managers will see the rationale as clearly as you do.
- Assume the users will remember it all – they won't touch it every day. As a result, ensure tools and materials are available for quick reference.
- Do it behind closed doors with a few key people!
- Keep it all 'behind the scenes' as it makes people feel like you are doing something sneaky.
- Expect anyone to fill in a form without guidance. If you do, they will fill it in as they think best with the wrong type of evidence in the wrong factor.
- Make it something just operated by reward people. Put HR business partners in the middle of it.
- Where a system is non-analytical don't oversell the ability to justify placement of roles, particularly in industries that employ large nu mbers of analytical professionals.

Procedures and policies

Appeals procedure

The appeals procedure should set out:

- the grounds upon which an appeal can be made, eg that an individual believes that he or she has been undergraded;

- the body that should hear the appeal, often a specially constituted appeals panel whose members should not have been involved in the original evaluation;

- the procedure for hearing the appeal, for example obtaining supporting evidence from the appellant, requesting a rationale from the original evaluation panel for their decision, or requesting a re-evaluation by the original panel (or by a specially formed panel);

- what happens if the appeals panel rejects the appeal – it is usual to make a hearing of that panel the final stage in the appeals procedure but typically provision is made for individuals who are still dissatisfied to take the issue up through the standard grievance procedure.

Protection policy

A protection policy indicates how the pay of employees will be safeguarded following the introduction of a new pay structure when some employees are likely to be over-graded and therefore overpaid. The policy will guarantee that in those circumstances employees will not suffer a loss of pay and they will thus be paid at a higher level than the size of the job and internal relativities justifies. They are then said to be 'red-circled', but they may be required to 'mark time', ie remain at the same rate until their pay is at the correct level for their grade.

Organizations have sometimes provided 'indefinite protection' to red-circled employees, ie maintaining the difference between current pay and range maximum for as long as the employee remains in the job. To differentiate them from employees paid in accordance with the pay scale they are sometimes placed on what is called a 'personal to job holder' scale. But this is undesirable, first because it will create permanent anomalies and, second because, when there are a lot of men in this situation, it will perpetuate unacceptable gender gaps.

Because of these considerations, the most common approach is to provide for red-circled employees to receive pay protection for a limited period, typically between two and four years. During this time the organization can choose to freeze the individual's salary or to give cost of living increases. The benefit to the organization of freezing salary is that the individual's pay is more likely to fall back within the grade range during the period of protection than if they receive a cost of living award. However, this can be regarded as unduly harsh, so many organizations still provide for the payment of 'across the board' cost of living awards during the protection period.

Assimilation policy

An assimilation policy deals with how employees should be placed into a new pay structure resulting from job evaluation. There are four categories of staff to be covered by the policy as explained below.

1. Current pay and pay potential both within the new pay range

The majority of employees will normally be in this category and the policy should be that they will not be given an increase in pay.

2. Current pay within the new pay range but pay potential higher than new maximum

In this case, if progression to the previous maximum was based on service only, ie a scale of annual increases to the maximum that is guaranteed to those who perform effectively, then this guarantee should be honoured or bought out. If as a result of honouring a pre-existing commitment a person's pay passes the maximum for the new grade, this should be treated as a 'red-circle' situation. If progression to the old maximum was not guaranteed, but was based on performance or contribution, then the new range maximum should normally be applied. Care will be needed to ensure that this does not adversely affect any specific category of staff, particularly female staff.

3. Current pay below the minimum for the new grade

This situation should be rectified as quickly as possible by raising the pay to the minimum of the new pay range. This should normally be the first call on any money allocated for assimilation. If the total cost of rectifying underpayments is more than the organization can afford, it may be necessary, however unpalatable, to 'green-circle' the person and phase the necessary increases, say one portion in the current year and the rest the next year – it is undesirable to phase increases over a longer period unless the circumstances are exceptional.

4. Current pay above the maximum for the new grade

This category usually includes either a high proportion of people who have been in their current job for a long time and who may have benefited from a lax approach to pay management in the past, or individuals who have received additional market-related payments or allowances that will no longer apply under the new pay scheme. They have to be 'red-circled' and dealt with in accordance with a protection policy.

Reference

e-reward (2017) *Job Evaluation Survey*, Stockport, e-reward

Job analysis 06

Formal job evaluation is based on the information provided by a job description or role profile, which is prepared by means of job analysis. As described in this chapter the analysis is conducted through either structured interviews or questionnaires.

Job descriptions

Traditional job descriptions contain an overview of the job and its place in the organization structure followed by detailed descriptions of duties and responsibilities. When used to inform analytical job evaluation they should not attempt to describe the duties in too much detail. They should instead sum up the main activities briefly. They should also include an analysis of the job demands in terms of each of the factors or elements in the scheme.

If the organization already has job descriptions in place they may possibly provide a basis for evaluation. But existing descriptions are often inadequate, out of date, and unusable because they have not been written to a consistent format. Moreover, they will typically not support a point-factor or analytical matching process. It is therefore almost always necessary to start afresh by deciding on a new standard format and conducting a job analysis programme.

Table 6.1 is an example of a role profile prepared for a job evaluation exercise.

Structured interviews

A structured interview is one that is based on a defined framework within which there is a set of predetermined questions. The purpose

Table 6.1   Example of a role profile

Job title	Accounts Assistant
Responsible to	Financial Accountant
Responsible to job holder	None
Overall purpose of job	To carry out processing of financial data
Key activities	• Process payments and invoices accurately • Verify calculations and input computer codes for a variety of documents • Check ledgers, statements and accounts to identify errors and take any necessary corrective action, referring more complex items to financial accountant • Maintain accurate financial records including data input to computer • Produce routine reports as required • Respond to customer enquiries and complaints
	Knowledge and skills (general)	• Knowledge of accounts procedures • Computer and keyboard skills • Communication skills – dealing with queries and writing routine reports
	Interpersonal skills	• Work well with others in office • Deal with difficult customers
	Judgement and decision-making	• Evaluates data to indicate any actions required • Makes decisions on the basis of readily available data • Refers more complex problems to financial accountant
Factor analysis	Complexity	• The work is quite diverse – processing and analysing data, preparing reports and dealing with queries • However, all aspects of the work are closely connected
	Responsibility for resources	• No responsibility for resources other than office equipment required to carry out the work

is to obtain the relevant facts about the job, namely the job title, organizational details (reporting relationships as described in an organization chart), a list of the tasks or duties performed by the job holder, and information about the level of the responsibilities involved and the demands made upon the job holder. The latter can cover the amount of supervision received, the degree of discretion allowed in making decisions, the typical problems to be solved, the amount of guidance available when solving the problems, the relative difficulty of the tasks to be performed, and the qualifications and skills required to carry out the work.

Job analysis interviews may be held with job holders but there is much to be said for interviewing the job holder's manager as well in order to check on the information supplied by the job holder. The same sequence of questions can be used and, although time-consuming, such checks can increase the accuracy of the analysis.

Conducting a job analysis interview

The steps required to conduct a structured job analysis interview are:

1 Define in advance the information required and how the interview will be structured.

2 Decide on a logical sequence of questions that are likely to elicit that information. These will consist of questions to establish job content and, for an analytical scheme, questions to find out the level of demands made on job holders in each of the factors used in the job evaluation scheme. Examples of questions are given below.

3 When conducting the interview be prepared to vary the predetermined structure of questions if it is necessary to explore aspects of the job more thoroughly or unexpected features of the work emerge.

4 Probe as necessary to establish what people really do – answers to questions are often vague and information may be given by means of untypical instances.

5 Ensure that job holders are not allowed to get away with vague or inflated descriptions of their work – they would not be human if they did not present the job in the best possible light.

6 Remember that if the factor plan for the job evaluation scheme has been published, which it should have been, the job holder or the job holder's manager may be aware of the factors that may contribute to a higher-level evaluation and adjust the information they supply accordingly.

7 Sort out the wheat from the chaff; answers to questions may produce a lot of irrelevant data that must be sifted before preparing the job description.

8 Obtain a clear statement from job holders about their authority to make decisions and the amount of guidance they receive from their manager or team leader and check this with the latter.

9 Avoid asking leading questions that make the expected answer obvious.

10 Allow the job holder ample opportunity to talk by creating an atmosphere of trust.

Job content questions

The following are typical basic questions on job content that may be put to job holders:

1 What is the title of your job?

2 To whom are you responsible?

3 Who is responsible to you? An organization chart is helpful.

4 What is the main purpose of your job in overall terms, ie what are you expected to do?

5 What are the key activities you have to carry out in your job? Try to group them under no more than eight headings.

6 For each of these activities, what authority do you have to decide what to do or how to do it?

7 What are you expected to know to be able to carry out your job?

8 What skills should you have to carry out your job?

These are the basic questions and supplementary ones may almost certainly be needed to get the information required, for example when dealing with questions five to eight.

The answers to these questions may need to be sorted out – they can often result in a mass of jumbled information that has to be analysed so that the various activities can be distinguished and refined to seven or eight key areas and the factors linked to those activities can be identified.

Factor level questions

Factor level questions such as the examples given below can be formulated by referring to the factor plan. In each case supplementary questions may have to be asked. Wherever possible, examples of what is involved should be obtained.

Knowledge and skills (general)

To what extent do any of the following statements apply to your job? The job involves:

- The application of specific administrative or technical skills.
- The application of a range of professional, specialist, technical, administrative or operational areas of knowledge and skills.
- The application of high levels of professional, specialist, technical or administrative expertise.
- The application of authoritative expertise in a key area of the organization's activities.

Interpersonal skills

To what extent do any of the following statements apply to your job? The job requires:

- The skills to exert some influence over others, getting them to accept a proposal or point of view.
- The skills to frequently relate to people inside and outside the organization, providing advice and guidance, dealing with problems affecting people and exerting influence on important matters. The skills may be used in negotiations and joint problem solving on relatively straightforward issues.
- The skills to relate constantly to people at senior levels inside and outside the organization.

- The skills to deal with internal and external contacts at high levels, handling important and non-routine issues and involving the exercise of considerable persuasive ability, sensitivity to others and tact. The skills may be used when conducting important negotiations, dealing with difficult and sensitive cases or acting as the recognized representative of the company on key issues externally.

Complexity

To what extent do any of the following statements apply to your job?

- There is some diversity in the work, which involves a number of non-routine elements and the exercise of a variety of skills although they are quite closely related to one another.
- The work is diverse, consisting of a number of different elements which are only broadly related to one another.
- The work is highly diverse, involving many different elements which may not be closely related to one another and the exercise of a wide variety of skills.
- The work is multi-disciplinary and involves making a broad range of highly diverse decisions

Responsibility for resources

To what extent do any of the following statements apply to your job?

- Leads a small team, and/or manages a small budget or is responsible for a range of facilities or equipment.
- Leads a large team or department of more than 10 people, and/or acts as budget manager for a department or office.
- Leads a major function or range of activities and manages a commensurately sized budget.

Advantages and disadvantages of interviewing

The advantages of the interviewing method are that it is flexible, can provide in-depth information and is easy to organize and prepare. It is therefore the most common approach. But interviewing can be time-consuming, which is why in large job analysis exercises, questionnaires may be used to provide advance information about the job. This speeds up the interviewing process or even replaces the interview altogether, although this means that much of the 'flavour' of the job – ie what it is really like – may be lost.

Written questionnaire

Increasingly organizations are attracted by a questionnaire-based approach rather than using job descriptions or role profiles because embarking on a complete rewrite of the organization's job descriptions may seem to be a formidable and time-consuming task. Instead a questionnaire may be used, with a commitment to review the design of job descriptions or role profiles on completion of the job evaluation project, using the information drawn from the questionnaires.

A typical questionnaire asks for narrative responses to questions that relate to each factor, evaluation criterion or element in the matching matrix. They may be given to employees for completion on the basis that they know best how the job is done, or to the line manager or, ideally, to both as a shared task to complete. An example of a questionnaire is given in Appendix C.

The risk of giving the questionnaire directly to job holders is that it allows for individuals to 'talk up' their roles, ie exaggerate the levels of responsibility etc involved. For this reason it is better to validate the completed questionnaire in discussion with the line manager, or to get the manager and job holder to complete the questionnaire together. Where there are multiple job holders it can be helpful to get a group of them together to generate the questionnaire responses, ideally using a facilitator to support the process, whilst allowing individuals to comment on any individual variation from the common responses.

Another approach to gathering evaluation information through questionnaires is by using a multiple choice-type questionnaire rather than obtaining a written description of the job. The questions may be based directly on the factor levels in a factor plan. This approach is used by some proprietary schemes. The questionnaire may even ask the completer of the questionnaire (typically either the job holder or manager) to make a tick against the appropriate factor level for the job. There are risks in this method because the individual is effectively evaluating the job, without any knowledge of the context. If the options are written in terms of the factor level descriptions the language can appear quite abstract to a job holder and they may feel that they have not been given sufficient opportunity to describe their job. Also, a multiple-choice questionnaire is unlikely to give enough background context about a job to be able to validate whether all the characteristics of a job are being picked up – although this may not be a problem if accurate good job descriptions or role profiles exist.

Written questionnaires may be used to speed up evaluations for a scheme that has been fully developed and tested but they are unlikely to be a satisfactory tool for use when developing a scheme.

Computer-aided analysis

Interactive computer-aided systems use a set of online questions. This enables a more sophisticated questioning approach whereby job holders are asked questions that relate directly to their job, rather than all the questions embedded in the scheme. If the same initial question on a factor is answered differently, the next question that appears will be different. This approach does not rely on job descriptions. An output of the interview is likely to be some form of job profile based on the interviewee's answers.

However, when developing a scheme, it is likely that the initial design of the 'paper' scheme will use a more traditional questionnaire approach in order to test the factors before building these into the computer tool.

The parties involved in job analysis

The parties involved in job analysis may be:

- *The job holder* who knows how the job is done in practice.
- *The job holder's manager* who should have an overview of what is required of the job holder.

- *The manager's manager* who may be used in a signing-off capacity or to resolve any differences between the job holder and their manager.

- *A trained analyst* who may interview job holders, facilitate discussions between the job holder and line manager, and help to resolve differences; analysts may be drawn from the project team, the HR function or a broader group of trained employees.

- *Trade union representatives* who may be involved as observers to the job analysis process, or sit in on interviews if requested by the job holder(s).

Whoever is involved will need to be given guidance or formally trained. This will include guidance on how to conduct interviews or complete/verify questionnaires, the need to distinguish between individual performance and the job requirements, and awareness training on how to avoid discrimination.

PART TWO
Job evaluation schemes and market pricing

Point-factor rating 07

Point-factor schemes are the most common forms of analytical job evaluation. They were used by 70 per cent of those with job evaluation schemes who responded to the 2017 e-reward job evaluation survey. This chapter explains the basic methodology and the main features of such schemes and describes how they should be designed. Examples are given at the end of the chapter.

Methodology

The methodology of point-factor schemes is to break down jobs into factors or key elements representing the demands made by the job on job holders. It is assumed that each of the factors will contribute to the value of the job and is an aspect of all the jobs to be evaluated but to different degrees. A point-factor scheme can be operated manually – a 'paper' scheme – or computers can be used to aid the evaluation process as described in Chapter 2 and further on in this chapter.

Each factor is divided into a hierarchy of levels. Definitions of these levels are produced to provide guidance on deciding the degree to which the factor applies in the job to be evaluated.

A maximum points score is allocated to each factor. The scores available may vary between different factors in accordance with beliefs about their relative significance. This is termed explicit weighting. If the number of levels varies between factors this means that they are implicitly weighted because the range of scores available will be greater in the factors with more levels.

The total score for a factor is divided between the levels to produce the numerical factor scale. Progression may be arithmetic, eg 50, 100,

150, 200 etc or geometric, eg 50, 100, 175, 275 etc. In the latter case, more scope is given to recognize the more senior jobs with higher scores.

The complete scheme consists of the factor and level definitions and the scoring system (the total score available for each factor and distributed to the factor levels). This comprises the 'factor plan'.

Jobs are 'scored' (ie allocated points) under each factor heading on the basis of the level of the factor in the job. This is done by comparing the features of the job with regard to that factor with the factor level definitions to find out which definition provides the best fit. The separate factor scores are then added together to give a total score that indicates the relative value of each job and can be used to place the jobs in rank order.

An example of a point-factor scheme is given in Appendix B.

Job evaluation factors

Job evaluation factors are the characteristics or key elements of jobs that are used to analyse and evaluate them in an analytical job evaluation scheme. Although many of the job evaluation factors used in different organizations capture similar job elements (this is an area where there are some enduring truths), the task of identifying and agreeing factors can be challenging.

There are six main categories of job evaluation factors:

1 The combination of the skills, knowledge and expertise that the employee needs to do the job.

2 The thinking challenges of the job, for example planning, analysis, decision making and problem solving.

3 Interpersonal skills, including leadership, communication and relationship building.

4 The responsibilities that the job has for resources, eg human, financial or physical resources.

5 The kinds of impact that the role has, either on internal operational effectiveness or on the external customer or environment.

6 The environmental, emotional or physical demands that are made in a job, for example difficult working conditions, involvement in dealing with challenging behaviour, pressures on those with caring responsibilities, or operational dexterity.

Within these six areas there are many different ways in which jobs can be described. This will depend on the extent to which the organization wants to express jobs in terms of responsibility or the effects of the job on the organization, or in terms of the 'inputs' that a job requires, ie what combination of applied knowledge, skills or behaviours (competencies). For example, many organizations include a factor relating to communication skills in their scheme. However, one organization may define this as the interpersonal skills needed to build relationships; another might place emphasis on the level and type of internal or external contacts that the job is required to have; yet another might focus on core verbal and oral communication skills required at different levels.

Respondents to the 2017 e-reward survey listed 29 factors between them but the most frequently used ones were:

1 knowledge and skills;

2 decision making;

3 impact;

4 people management;

5 interpersonal skills.

The factor plan

The factor plan is the key job evaluation document. It defines each of the selected factors and the levels within them and guides evaluators in making decisions about the levels of demand and responsibility present in a job. The basic number of levels (often four, five, six or seven) has to reflect the range of responsibilities and demands in the jobs covered by the scheme. An example of the definition of a factor with five levels is given in Table 7.1.

Table 7.1   Example of factor level definitions

Judgement and decision making: the requirement to exercise judgement in making decisions and solving problems, including the degree to which the work involves choice of action or creativity.
1   The work is well defined and relatively few new situations are encountered. The causes of problems are readily identifiable and can be dealt with easily.
2   Evaluation of information is required to deal with occasional new problems and situations and to decide on a course of action from known alternatives. Occasionally required to participate in the modification of existing procedures and practices.
3   Exercises discriminating judgement in dealing with relatively new or unusual problems where a wide range of information has to be considered and the courses of action are not obvious. May fairly often be involved in devising new solutions.
4   Frequently exercises independent judgement when faced with unusual problems and situations where no policy guidelines or precedents are available. May also frequently be responsible for devising new strategies and approaches, which require the use of imagination and ingenuity.
5   Deals with widely differing problems calling for extreme clarity of thought in assessing conflicting information and balancing the risks associated with possible solutions. Additionally, one of the main requirements of the role may be to develop fundamentally new strategies and approaches.

The total points score is allocated to each factor and distributed between each level as in the example shown in Table 7.2.

This is described as an unweighted factor plan. The scoring system is an example of even (arithmetical) progression. Each step increases by the same number of points. But weighting and scoring systems can vary, as described below.

Factor weighting

Weighting is the process of attaching more importance to some factors than others. An unweighted factor plan is one in which the factors are treated as being equally important and the maximum number of

Table 7.2 Example of an unweighted factor plan with arithmetical score progression

	Levels				
Factor	1	2	3	4	5
Knowledge and skills (general)	20	70	70	80	100
Interpersonal skills	20	70	70	80	100
Judgement and decision-making	20	70	70	80	100
Complexity	20	70	70	80	100
Responsibility for resources	20	70	70	80	100

points is the same for each of them. The 2017 e-reward survey of job evaluation found that 39 per cent of the respondents had unweighted schemes. Where weighting is used there are two types:

1 *Explicit weighting*, in which the maximum points available for what are regarded as more important factors increase.

2 *Implicit weighting*, in which some factors have more levels than others but the same scoring progression per level exists as in the other factors. The factors with more levels would have more points available to them and would have therefore been implicitly weighted.

Explicit weighting is the most popular approach. It was adopted by 77 per cent of the respondents to the 2017 e-reward survey. Implicit weighting was used by only 17 per cent of respondents.

The number and choice of factors may also implicitly weight a scheme. If two factors that would normally be treated as being of equal importance are compressed into one then implicit weighting of that combined factor has taken place, ie it is undervalued in terms of its significance.

Scoring progression

The scoring progression within each factor can take place in two ways. The 'arithmetic' or linear approach assumes that there are consistent step differences between factor levels, as illustrated in

Table 7.2. There may be a single score for each level as shown above or a range of scores to give a measure of choice. But most schemes have only a single score to recognize that scoring judgements are insufficiently accurate to be expressed along a scale within a factor. Judging which factor is appropriate is hard enough.

Alternatively, geometric scoring assumes that there are progressively larger score differences at each successive level in the hierarchy to reflect progressive increases in responsibility. This is illustrated in the example of a weighted factor plan in Table 7.3.

The rank order produced by either of these scoring methods is unlikely to differ much, but it can be argued that the greater 'distance' between level scores in geometric progression reflects an increasing gap between job requirements at the top end of the hierarchy. It can also indicate clearer breaks between grades when it comes to designing the structure.

Table 7.3 Example of a weighted factor plan with geometric score progression

	Levels				
Factor	**1**	**2**	**3**	**4**	**5**
1 Expertise	20	50	90	170	200
2 Responsibility	15	35	75	105	170
3 Problem solving	15	35	75	105	170
4 Relationships	15	35	75	105	170
5 Impact	20	50	90	170	200

Designing a point-factor job evaluation scheme

The following steps are required to design a point-factor scheme. Methods of introducing such a scheme were described in Chapter 5. It is best to set up a project team consisting of managers and staff representatives to carry out the design with guidance from HR and, if possible, an external consultant. It is advisable to brief them thoroughly on the principles of job evaluation and what the project team will be expected to do.

Step 1: Select and define factors

The guidelines for selecting factors are:

1 The number of factors should not exceed 12 or so otherwise the scheme would become too complex. Many schemes have no more than five or six factors, which can be sufficient.

2 The factors must be capable of identifying the relevant and significant features of jobs in order to support the assessment of the similarities or differences between them.

3 The factor definitions should be clear, relevant and understandable and written in a way that is meaningful to those who will use the scheme.

4 The factors should reflect the values of the organization.

5 They should apply equally well to different types of work including specialists and generalists, lower-level and higher-level jobs.

6 The whole range of jobs to be evaluated at all levels should be covered without favouring any particular job or occupation.

7 The scheme should fairly measure features of female-dominated jobs as well as male-dominated jobs.

8 The choice should not lead to discrimination on the grounds of gender, race, disability, religion or age, or against anyone in one of the LGBT+ categories. Experience should not be included as a factor because it could be discriminatory either on the grounds of gender or age. The same principle applies to education or qualifications as stand-alone factors.

9 Job features frequently found in jobs carried out mainly by one gender should not be omitted, for example manual dexterity, interpersonal skills and 'caring' responsibilities. If such features are included, it is important that the scheme captures the range of skills across all jobs, including those that might be dominated by another gender.

10 Double counting should be avoided, ie each factor must be independent of every other factor – the more factors (or sub-factors) in the plan, the higher the probability that double counting will take place.

11 Elision or compression of more than one significant job feature under a single factor heading should be avoided. If important factors are compressed with others it means that they could be undervalued.

12 The factors should be acceptable to those who will be covered by the scheme.

The following sources of information and approaches to support the selection of factors are available.

Reviewing internal strategy/business documents

Looking through existing written materials such as organization or human resources strategy documents can give an insight into the current values and language.

Reviewing people related frameworks or processes

In the past, job evaluation criteria were not necessarily linked to other human resources processes or frameworks. However, many organizations have now accepted the need to adopt a more coherent approach by applying the organization's values and language across related processes. Reviewing existing job descriptions may be a place to start.

The most obvious potential link is with an organization's competency framework, as many of the concepts reflected in competencies are similar to job evaluation criteria, albeit expressed in behavioural or skills-based language. The extent to which a link can be made with an existing competency framework will depend on how it has been defined. It will be easier to do where the competencies are skills related to job requirements, eg business acumen (job-centric) rather than person-oriented, eg tenacity (person-centric). The desirability of achieving a degree of linkage was a finding from the e-reward survey, and was one of the main reasons for companies favouring a tailor-made scheme.

Interviews with line managers and other stakeholders

Discussions with key managers can help to get an early perspective on the senior management priorities for the scheme. This group is most likely to have a view about the future demands on the organization and what work will be valued. Early senior manager involvement can also help to dispel myths and misconceptions about job evaluation, and will support the overall communications process – particularly if the managers concerned are those who will later be responsible for approving the scheme.

Focus groups

Structured meetings with employees can be a good way of understanding what aspects of jobs are currently valued and what people think are the most important. Such meetings can also contribute to achieving better involvement and communications. Because employees may be unfamiliar with job evaluation concepts, the agenda will normally need to cover an overview of what job evaluation is, the rationale for introducing job evaluation, what the factors are, and what makes a 'good' factor. Views can be explored on possible factors. Focus groups can also be used to obtain the views of employees about how the scheme should be communicated.

Focus groups can be particularly useful for organizations with geographically or functionally diverse constituencies or for developing sector-wide schemes. In developing the UK further education scheme focus groups were run in about a dozen colleges around the country. They were selected to represent different types of institution as well as geographic diversity. The focus groups generated a long list of possible factor headings, which showed a high degree of consistency across the institutions. This input was clustered into 10 main groups, which became the factors.

Consideration should also be given to whether input from other stakeholders is helpful. Where a scheme is to be jointly agreed with trade unions their representatives should be involved at an early stage. Staff groups can also be consulted. A voluntary organization may want to include volunteers in focus groups, or to obtain the views of key trustees.

Project team input

A project team set up to develop the job evaluation scheme can explore possible factors in a number of ways, for example:

- Open discussion – drawing on the inputs that are available to the team from other sources.

- Selecting a number of jobs/roles and exploring the differences between them – what makes one 'bigger' or 'smaller' than another. This can be done informally or through a process such as whole-job ranking or paired comparison.

- Using an existing database or list of common factor headings, posting these up on a flipchart and drawing out and clustering the job dimensions that seem most relevant to the organization; if a consultant is being used, this exercise is likely to use headings from their factor database.

Step 2: Define factor levels

A decision has to be made on the number of levels required (eg four, five, six or seven). This has to reflect the range of responsibilities and demands in the jobs covered by the scheme.

The starting point can be an analysis of what would character-ize the highest or lowest level for each factor and how these should be described. For example, the highest level in a judgement and decision-making factor could be defined as: 'Deals with widely differing problems calling for extreme clarity of thought in assessing conflicting information and balancing the risks associated with possi-ble solutions. Additionally, one of the main requirements of the role may be to develop fundamentally new strategies and approaches.' The lowest level could be defined as: 'The work is well defined and relatively few new situations are encountered. The causes of prob-lems are readily identifiable and can be dealt with easily.'

It might then be decided that there should be three levels between the highest and lowest level on the basis that this truly reflects the graduation in responsibilities or demands. The outcome would then be the definition of the factor and each of the five levels as illustrated in Table 7.1. This process is repeated for each factor.

The following guidelines should be used in defining levels:

1 Each level should be defined as clearly as possible to help evalua-tors make 'best fit' decisions.

2 The levels should cover the whole range of demands in this factor that are likely to arise in the jobs with which the evaluation scheme is concerned.

3 The link between the content of level definitions should be related specifically to the definition of the factor concerned and should not overlap with other factors.

4 There should be uniform progression in the definitions level by level from the lowest to the highest level. There should be no gaps or undefined intermediate levels which might lead to evaluators finding it difficult to be confident about the allocation of a level of demand. Some schemes have undefined interim levels. This is only likely to work where there are clear steps in demand between the defined levels and where there are protocols on how to use the undefined levels.

5 The factor levels should represent clear and recognisable steps in responsibility and the demands made on jobholders.

6 The levels should be defined in absolute, not relative terms. They should not rely upon a succession of undefined comparatives, eg small, medium, large. So far as possible any dimensions should be defined.

7 Each level definition should stand on its own. Level definitions should not be defined by reference to a lower or higher level, ie it is insufficient to define a level in words to the effect that it is a higher (or lower) version of an adjacent level.

There is a limit to the number of words that can be included in a factor level definition (too many confuse rather than clarify) and the words themselves cannot always convey accurate meanings. For example, a Level 3 definition for a planning and organization factor may refer to 'planning and organization of a number of complex activities'. But this does not tell the evaluator how many activities justify a Level 3 rating or what constitutes a 'complex' activity. What has to happen is that, as evaluators gain experience in interpreting the level definitions, they record conventions or protocols that help to achieve consistent evaluations by providing guidance on what these or similar words mean, preferably with quantitative examples illustrated by reference to benchmark jobs that have already been evaluated.

One of the main purposes of testing in a design program is to identify where conventions are necessary and ensure that they are made available to evaluators. But this process of developing conventions continues when the benchmark jobs are evaluated, which means that in a large job, project evaluators may have to revisit the conclusions reached in earlier stages of the programme and re-evaluate in the light of the conventions.

Step 3: Decide scoring system

The aim is to design a point-factor scheme that will operate fairly and consistently to produce a rank order of jobs, based on the total points score for each job. Each level in the factor plan has to be allocated a points value so that there is a scoring progression from the lowest to the highest level. There are no rules on what the maximum points should be as long as it is possible to discriminate between levels. The maximum for a factor is typically between 100 and 200.

A decision needs to be made on how to set the scoring progression within each factor. As explained earlier in this chapter, the choice is between two methods: (1) 'arithmetic' or (2) linear.

It is best to allocate a single finite score for each level because giving a choice from a range of scores can complicate evaluations. If it is decided that there should be some choice, this should be as simple as possible, for example low, standard and high. If this approach is used, protocols should be developed to explain what each step change means and it should be subject to thorough testing to ensure consistency.

Step 4: Decide on the factor weighting

A decision has to be made on whether the factors should be weighted or not and if so, whether weighting should be explicit or implicit. It is often assumed that weighting is desirable because it is necessary to recognize that the value of a job is likely to be affected more by some factors than others. But experience has shown that the initial choice of factors is more significant than weighting in determining the relative score of jobs. And decisions on weighting can be arbitrary and difficult to justify.

Approach to weighting

There should be a rationale for the weighting system, eg relative value of factors to the organization, agreed relative values – it should not just give the answers people want. Explicit weighting accords with the belief that some factors are more important than others. Implicit weighting is more likely to take place when there is a large number of factors – 10 or more – and the impact of explicitly weighting any factors is less (unless the weighting is so disproportionate that the non-weighted factors become immaterial).

Rather than rush into a weighting decision because it seems the right thing to do, consideration should be given to initially try out an unweighted scheme and test it as described in Step 7. But if it is felt strongly by the team that weighting is desirable then the design process would continue as indicated below. However, unless the scheme is to be weighted in favour of a factor that applies strongly to a specific area of work, the re-modelling of weightings is likely to yield fairly small changes in rank order as all jobs will be affected to the same degree by the re-weighting. Whatever approach to weighting is adopted, the results should be tested and if these are unacceptable, further testing can be undertaken using alternative forms of weighting.

Making weighting decisions – the judgemental method

Explicit weighting decisions are often judgemental although they can be based on agreed guiding principles (eg no factor will have a weighting of less than 5 per cent or more than 30 per cent). Decisions can be made by a job evaluation project team although discussions tend to be based on opinions and feelings. For example, it is often held that knowledge and skills or expertise are more important than anything else and must therefore be weighted. A typical method is to ask each member of the team to distribute 100 points amongst the factors. The distributions are then reproduced on a flip chart by the facilitator, who does not reveal their source. The team next discusses the distribution of suggested weightings and comes to a conclusion. Averaging the weightings should be avoided if possible. It is far better to reach a decision through consensus after a debate. This process is totally unscientific. It is essential, therefore, to make the initial weightings provisional and test them using the full weighted factor plan.

Implicit weighting decisions can be made when analysing the number of levels to be made available for each factor. A restricted range of levels might be adopted for one or more factors when the scope of the factor or factors is considered to be more limited than others, and the factors will thus have been implicitly weighted. But this is a matter of judgement, which can easily be subjective.

Making explicit weighting decisions – the statistical method

The statistical method of multiple regression analysis has been used in an attempt to make explicit weighting decisions more scientific. Multiple regression analysis measures the relationship between a number of variables to indicate how they affect one another. When applied to weighting, the aim is to find the weighting combination that will most closely replicate a predetermined rank order of jobs (the reference ranking). This ranking might be based on comparing the market rates of a number of benchmark jobs, paired comparisons of the benchmarks, or what is considered subjectively to be a fair ranking of the benchmark jobs ('felt-fair ranking', which is in accordance with the somewhat circular felt-fair principle originated by Elliott Jaques to the effect that if someone feels a payment system is fair then it is fair)

However, unless the reference ranking has itself been developed using an objective process, the regression analysis may simply reproduce the existing hierarchy, thus reinforcing inequalities or preconceptions. The use of market data is particularly suspect in this respect, as pay discrimination in favour of male-dominated roles may already be embedded in the market.

This step will complete the design of the draft factor plan.

Step 5: Select and analyse benchmark jobs

A sample of benchmark jobs should be identified. These will be used to test the factor plan and retained as ones for which external market rate comparisons can be made and as examples of jobs in each grade to assist in evaluation. They can also be used for matching on a job-to-job basis (see Chapter 8).

Benchmark jobs should represent each level in the organization and be chosen from each of the main functions. The proportion depends on the size and complexity of the organization; in a large organization it may be up to 10–15 per cent of the jobs if the organization is fairly simple, but it could be much higher in some complex organizations (30 per cent or more). The benchmark jobs are then analysed in terms of the factors.

Step 6: Evaluate benchmark jobs

The project team uses the factor plan to evaluate the benchmark jobs. Initial training sessions are helpful; the team practises making evaluations with the plan using made-up job profiles. One of the following three methods of evaluation can be used.

1. Factor by factor

The team takes each factor in turn and evaluates all jobs in respect of that factor, ie whole jobs are not evaluated in turn. This is the best method but it takes time. A factor-by-factor approach rather than a job-by-job approach means that panel members are less likely to make decisions on total scores based on *a priori* judgements about the relative value of the whole jobs, which they might find hard to change. Instead they are looking at responses for that factor in relation to responses for other jobs. They are more likely to focus on 'read-across' analytical judgements about the level of particular factors and it will be easier for them to refer for guidance to previous evaluations of the same factor in other benchmark jobs.

When there are variations in factor evaluations, individual panel members are asked to give reasons for their conclusions. But the facilitator or chair has to be careful not to allow them to be pressurized to change their views. If team members have been properly briefed and if there is a carefully designed, tested and understood factor plan and good information about the job, the extent to which evaluations vary is usually fairly limited, which enables consensus to be achieved more easily.

2. Whole jobs disclosed

Each panel member evaluates whole jobs factor by factor and then informs the panel of their conclusions. The facilitator records their separate views and then initiates a discussion with the objective of achieving consensus on the rating for each factor and therefore the overall score. This can be time-consuming because panel members may be influenced by pre-formed judgements and, having made up their minds, find it difficult to shift their ground. Again, time is saved if individual or pairs of panel members evaluate the jobs prior to the panel meeting, and the responses are collated on a spreadsheet. It also helps if the collated responses can be reviewed by panel members prior to the group meeting, as it will give time for the panel members to review their own responses in the light of any areas of difference.

3. Whole jobs undisclosed

This is a variation of the second approach where the whole panel is involved in evaluating each job. Each panel member evaluates whole jobs factor by factor but does not communicate their views formally to other members of the panel. Instead, the panel as a whole discusses and agrees the evaluation of each factor in turn to produce a total job evaluation score. This speeds up the evaluation and consensus can be easier to achieve because panel members are not put in the position of having to defend their prior judgements against all comers. But there is the danger of the weaker members of the panel allowing themselves to be swayed by strongly expressed majority views. This approach therefore only works with good facilitation that ensures that the discussion is not dominated by one or two powerful members and that all members have their say. Where the complete panel is evaluating jobs, some organizations start with the whole job disclosed method and when panel members (and the facilitator) become more experienced move on to the whole job undisclosed method.

Step 7: Test draft factor plan

No one ever gets a factor plan right first time. Even if a project team has already worked through two or three drafts of the plan, they are likely to come up with some changes or queries about relativities between statements, weighting and scoring systems.

The plan needs to be tested on the benchmark jobs. The fundamental aims of the test are to check on the extent to which the factor plan enables evaluators to produce sensible and acceptable results and to identify any improvements that need to be made to any of the plan's features. The clarity of the plan and the ease with which it can be used is also tested. The test can also begin the process of establishing conventions, which will be used to interpret the meaning of factor-level definitions.

Each benchmark job is evaluated and scored by the project team and then ranked according to the total score.

The project team then considers the extent to which it is believed the rank order is valid in the sense that the evaluations correctly indicate relative job value. There is no ideal method of doing this – no single, simple test that will establish the validity of a factor plan. The fact that it is difficult to prove that the results are valid is a major weakness of point-factor evaluation.

The following methods are available:

1 *Reference ranking* – the team compares the ranking produced by the job evaluation with the rank order produced by a ranking exercise. The technique of paired comparison (see Chapter 2) may be used to guide the ranking process. The problem with this approach is that the ranking may do no more than confirm existing relativities, which may not be appropriate.

2 *Hierarchy comparisons* – the rank order produced by the test is compared with the existing organizational hierarchy and any obvious discrepancies are investigated. However, care must be taken not to assume that the existing hierarchy is the correct one.

3 *External market test* – the internal rank order is compared with that existing in comparable jobs elsewhere. But this may reflect pay differentials between job families, rather than internal measures of job worth. It may also replicate existing inequities between male and female jobs.

4 *The 'felt-fair test'* – the rank order produced by the test is compared with what the job evaluation panel 'feels' is the fair and therefore

appropriate ranking. Discrepancies are then identified. A danger of this approach is that it is often based only on opinion and can simply reproduce existing prejudices and perpetuate existing anomalies. Inevitably, however, a 'felt-fair' approach is often adopted as the main method of testing the plan. It is therefore necessary to be particularly alert to the possibility of pre-judgements affecting opinions and to challenge any apparent move in that direction. One or more of the first three tests can be used for this purpose.

The more specific aims of the test are to establish the extent to which:

- the factors are appropriate;
- the factors cover all aspects of the jobs to be evaluated;
- the factors are non-discriminatory;
- the factors avoid double counting and are not compressed unduly;
- level definitions are worded clearly, graduated properly and cover the whole range of demands applicable to the jobs to be evaluated so that they provide good guidance on the allocation of factor levels to evaluators and thus enable consistent evaluations to be made;
- the scoring system is appropriate;
- weighting decisions are defensible.

Step 8: Confirm factor plan

Changes are made to the factor plan in the light of the test results. If there have been major changes another test will be required.

Possible conversion of a paper scheme to a computer-aided scheme

The steps set out above will produce a paper-based scheme, which is the most common approach. But converting the paper scheme to a computer-aided scheme can offer a number of advantages including greater consistency, speed and the elimination of much of the paperwork.

Computer-aided schemes use software provided by suppliers such as Pilat but if the job evaluation scheme is bespoke, it will typically be derived from the paper-based scheme. If a computer-aided scheme is adopted, the job evaluation project team or panel will not be required to spend time carrying out detailed paper evaluations but it is necessary to set up a review panel which can validate and agree the outcomes of the computer-aided process. A grading outcome is only as good as the job information that has been entered into the system and hard lessons have been learnt by organizations that have ended up with a 'fully automated' scheme but unacceptable outcomes.

Examples

Crown Prosecution Service

As a government agency, the Crown Prosecution Service (CPS) is obliged to use job evaluation, a policy initiated by the Treasury in 1992 to support job analysis and grading in the Civil Service. There are two different point-factor schemes: JEGS – Job Evaluation and Grading Support – is used for jobs up to and including grade 7 posts, and JESP – Job Evaluation for Senior Posts – is used for senior civil servants, ie all those on grade 5 posts (assistant director level) and above.

The CPS says that the most important reasons for using job evaluation are to ensure consistency of grades across the service and to establish the relative worth of the jobs. It also facilitates the accommodation of new or revised jobs into the grading structure and helps to avoid discrimination. JE therefore underpins all the organization's pay and performance initiatives.

Process

There is a job evaluation protocol, agreed between the trade unions and the CPS, which sets out under what circumstances a job will be evaluated and the requirements from employees, managers, the departmental trade unions and HR staff to ensure that the evaluation is accurate, objective and fair. All jobs are evaluated independently by HR and union representatives, and are then passed to a quality assurance panel, also consisting of representatives of HR and the unions who will determine the final assessment. There are trained evaluators around the country, although HR controls the process and policy centrally.

Roles are benchmarked against the public-sector labour market, and market analysis shows that the CPS pays upper quartile rates. Where there is conflict between internal equity and the market the CPS will sometimes pay supplements.

For new jobs, HR consults with the trade unions and produces a job description, person specification and an 'indicative' evaluation. Once the job holder has been in post for up to a year, the job holder fills out a job analysis form and the job is re-evaluated. A job may sometimes be advertised as a temporary grade, so that applicants are aware that it may change.

Dip sample

The streamlining process involves taking a dip sample, so that instead of interviewing everyone in a particular role, a sample of, say, 2.5 or 5 per cent of the population are asked to complete a job analysis form, and these are evaluated by the panel to establish the appropriate grade, which could be higher or lower than the existing grade. The sample is selected by gender, age, ethnicity and disability, to reflect the profile of the whole group.

Communication

The CPS recognizes that it is important to ensure that each step of the JE process and design is understood by all and that there is no room for different interpretations of what the design is trying to achieve. Involving the trade unions and training a pool of union representatives in the evaluation process makes it easier to get buy-in to changes in grades. The protocol agreed with the unions sets out details of the JE process and its scope. In addition, there is an easy-to-read process manual for staff and managers, which sets out the circumstances under which they can ask for a job to be evaluated.

Maintenance

The panel meets as and when needed. In general, however, job evaluation is a weekly activity, with new or changed jobs coming through regularly. It takes around an hour to carry out an indicative evaluation and about half a day to do a full evaluation. The process is fully computerized, which contributes to a speedy turnaround.

Civil Service JEGS and JESP schemes

Table 7.4   Civil Service JEGS and JESP schemes

	JEGS	JESP
Who does it cover?	All staff up to and including grade 7	Senior Civil Service (grade 5 – associate directors and above)
Factors	<ul><li>Knowledge and skills</li><li>Contacts and communications</li><li>Problem solving</li><li>Decision making</li><li>Autonomy</li><li>Management of resources</li><li>Impact</li></ul>	<ul><li>Managing people</li><li>Accountability</li><li>Judgement</li><li>Influencing</li><li>Professional competence (where appropriate)</li></ul>

Rencol Tolerance Rings

Rencol Tolerance Rings is an SME based in the UK. It is the only UK manufacturer of tolerance rings – industrial fasteners – and is unable to recruit in the external labour market for staff with product knowledge, so employee retention is a priority. Manual workers make up about 70 per cent of the workforce. Rencol is a non-union company, but consults extensively and has had a works council since 2005. It introduced a point-factor job evaluation scheme for all staff in 2007, largely at the behest of employees, many of whom believed their roles were undervalued.

The scheme was designed by a joint working party led by ACAS. Once the scheme had been designed and every job evaluated, a new seven-grade pay structure was constructed, with grade boundaries established where there were obvious gaps between clusters of jobs. Rencol is happy with what it has achieved, although in retrospect it says it would have taken a more strategic approach to the whole process, from embarking on JE to adopting new pay and progression arrangements.

Rencol's factors

- knowledge/experience (the most highly weighted factor)
- communication skills;
- handling information;
- physical skills;
- autonomy;
- responsibility for staff;
- responsibility for financial resources;
- responsibility for product and physical resources;
- working conditions.

The process

The original purpose of the scheme was to establish relativities between jobs that would be understood and perceived as fair by employees. And since it was employee feedback, expressed in opinion surveys, that prompted the adoption of job evaluation, the company believed that it was important that employees were involved. It asked ACAS to assist, and the ACAS facilitator helped to set up a joint working party to design a tailor-made point-factor scheme and take part in its implementation. The working party consisted of six people and the HR manager as an ex-officio member.

The company asked for volunteers and then picked people to represent different occupational areas and levels of responsibility within the business. It took around six weeks to train everyone involved and to evaluate some benchmark jobs, and another 12 weeks for all 50 jobs to be evaluated. Two panel members interviewed each job holder and completed a job analysis questionnaire. The job holder and their manager then reviewed the job analysis to ensure that nothing had been left out, and the factor points were added together to give a total for each job.

Although this had not been part of the original plan, it became obvious once all the jobs had been evaluated that the company needed to introduce a new grading structure. Before this, everyone had been on spot rates, which had developed without any rationale over the organization's 25-year history. A seven-grade structure was put in place and staff were informed about their new pay band, though not their individual JE scores. Grades were defined in terms of a range of points scores and jobs are placed in a grade if their score is within the range, but there is no link between an individual's pay and where they sit in the band.

Communication

The company holds monthly meetings to which all staff are invited, and these, together with a monthly newsletter, were used to keep everyone informed about the job evaluation process. Once the work was finished there was a full presentation at a monthly meeting and every employee received a letter telling them about their new grade. Employees reacted favourably and most felt that the JE exercise had come up with the right results.

Maintenance

The JE scheme is maintained on a rolling basis by the HR manager, who evaluates one job a week. He meets every job holder, or representative where several people do the same job, to review the job analysis. Where there have been any significant changes, the job is referred to the six-member panel, some of whom were involved in the original working party. New jobs are also referred to the panel. The full JE process is used in every case.

Equity and other problems

When a job is about to be filled or a new job created, it is benchmarked against the external market. Only after this is it evaluated, because the evaluation process is based on the experiences of the person doing the job. That person may not be fully aware of all the demands of the job so the situation can arise that the internal JE score and grade is below their market rate. Even though this is dealt with through market rate supplements, the company is still concerned by what it sees as a problem of internal equity. In addition, existing staff were assimilated to the nearest point on the new pay structure, which also means that person A may be earning less than person B who has more responsibility but is lower down the grade.

Rencol is aware that there is a temptation for managers to add responsibilities to a job to get the post holder some extra money.

Rencol's dos and don'ts

Table 7.5   Rencol's dos and don'ts

Dos	Don'ts
• Ensure that you use a balanced, cross-functional team • Communicate well with all employees, both collectively and individually • Review each analysis, at least on an annual basis	• Give undue weight to one particular factor as this may distort the outcome • Publish individual scores • Assume that because nobody has said anything a job hasn't changed

Stockport Council

Stockport Council started to use job evaluation in 1990: Hay for managers and the Greater London Whitley Council scheme for white-collar employees. But in 1997 a national agreement was reached to implement Single Status in England and Wales, that is, the harmonization of the terms and conditions of former manual workers and APT&C employees. This required a single job evaluation system for white-collar and manual workers. Along with most other councils in the UK, Stockport moved cautiously towards Single Status because of the problem of having to equalize the earnings of male manual workers who have traditionally received bonuses and female workers who have not.

The Greater London Whitley Council JE scheme could only be used for white-collar employees, so, for the last year, the council has been working with the trade unions to implement the Greater London Provincial Council (GLPC) JE scheme, which can be used for all employees, although Stockport is retaining Hay for managers. Jobs on the borders of the two JE schemes are being looked at carefully to ensure that someone at the top of the GLPC scheme would not earn more if they were evaluated through Hay, and vice versa.

Process

When introducing the new scheme, Stockport sought to build on the existing job descriptions and evaluations and evaluated a further 80 benchmark jobs across all the non-managerial occupational groups. Panels consisted of equal numbers of union and management representatives, all of whom had been trained in union methodology. The manager of the role being evaluated attends the meeting as an expert witness, but leaves the meeting once they have answered questions about the job.

There has been a long history of job evaluation in the organization, and there is general acceptance that the process is fair. Despite this, it has in some cases been difficult to get agreement on job content between the employee and their manager. Managers have been urged to 'evaluate for the future', that is, to think about future challenges and incorporate them into job descriptions.

Communication

Managers have been kept informed about the progress of the new scheme through the HR bulletin, which is circulated every six to eight weeks. A specific communications exercise focused on the employees who currently receive a bonus, some of whom will be going into pay protection arrangements; they have all received a face-to-face briefing and individual letters explaining what is happening.

Advice

Stockport Council suggests the following 'dos' and 'don'ts'.

'Do':

- consider how your proposed scheme will fit into your particular organization;
- consult and communicate widely and prepare the organization for major changes in pay relativities;
- ensure you have sufficient time and resources in place to do the job properly.

'Don't':

- underestimate the amount of time and effort involved in job evaluation activity;

- let it be perceived as purely an HR initiative;
- evaluate for the past. Ensure your scheme takes on board service modernization.

Greater London Provincial Council job evaluation scheme factors

Supervision/management of people – 7 levels
Assesses the scope of managerial duties and the nature of the work which is supervised. Accounts for flexible working patterns, deputizing, the number of staff supervised and their geographical dispersal.

Creativity and innovation – 7 levels
Measures the extent to which the work requires innovative and imaginative responses to issues and in the resolution of problems, and the impact of guidelines.

Contacts and relationships – 8 levels
Examines the content and environment of contacts required as part of the job. Measures the range and outcome of contacts.

Decisions
Operates as two sub-factors:

- *Discretion* – 7 levels – identifies freedom to act and the controls in place.
- *Consequences* – 5 levels – measures the outcome of decisions by effect, range and timescale.

Resources – 5 levels
Assesses the personal and identifiable responsibility for resources.

Work environment

Work demands – 5 levels
Considers the relationship between work programmes, goals, deadlines and the subsequent management of priorities.

Physical demands – 7 levels

Identifies a range of postures and demands of a physical nature.

Working conditions – 7 levels

Examines the typical elements encountered with working inside and outside.

Work context – 7 levels

Examines the potential health and safety risks to employees carrying out their duties.

Knowledge and skill – 8 levels

Assesses the depth and breadth of knowledge and skills required. This factor is the most highly weighted.

References

e-reward (2017) *Job Evaluation Survey*, Stockport, e-reward
Jaques, E (1961) *Equitable Payment*, London, Heinemann

Matching

08

Matching is the process of evaluating a job by establishing the extent to which its characteristics are similar to those set out in grade or level definition (job-to-grade matching), or to a description of the characteristics of another job (job-to-job matching). In job-to-grade matching, when a reasonably good fit is established between a job and the definition of a particular grade or level in a structure, the job is allocated to or 'slotted' into that grade. In job-to-job matching, when it is established that the characteristics of a job to be evaluated are similar to those of another job that has already been evaluated (a benchmark job), the job under review is allocated to the same grade or is eligible for the same rate of pay as the benchmark job.

Matching can be analytical or non-analytical. This chapter includes descriptions of matching schemes and their development. Matching was formerly known as job classification.

Job-to-grade analytical matching

In job-to grade analytical matching, jobs are analysed and described in terms of a set of job evaluation factors as in a conventional point-factor scheme. This leads to the production of a job description, often called a job or role profile to distinguish it from a conventional job description which simply sets out the main tasks carried out by the job holder. A grade or level structure is developed consisting of a sequence or hierarchy of grades or levels that have been defined analytically with the same set of factors used in the job profiles. The job profiles are then compared factor by factor with the range of grade or level profiles to establish which grade provides the best match and thus grade the job.

An analytical matching system can be underpinned by a traditional point-factor scheme that supplies the factors but also defines each band in terms of a points range by means of the evaluation of a representative selection of benchmark jobs. When a job cannot readily be matched to any grade the point-factor scheme is used to evaluate it and establish the points range and therefore grade to which the job belongs.

Job-to-job analytical matching

In job-to-job analytical matching, profiles for jobs to be evaluated are matched analytically against a set of common factors or elements with benchmark job profiles. A benchmark job is one that has already been graded as a result of an initial job evaluation exercise. It is used as a point of reference with which other jobs can be compared and valued. Thus, if benchmark role A has been evaluated and placed in grade 3 and there is a good fit between the factor profile of role B and that of role A, then role B will also be placed in grade 3. Generic role profiles, ie those covering a number of like roles, will be used for any class or cluster of roles with essentially the same range of responsibilities such as team leaders or personal assistants. Job-to-job matching may be used in combination with job-to-grade matching.

Job-to-job matching can be used on its own or it can be applied as a supplement to job-to-grade matching. This functions as a check on the job-to-grade match or an alternative if that type of match is difficult. Benchmark jobs can provide an additional method of defining or illustrating a grade definition or profile.

Non-analytical matching

This approach is based on a definition of the number and characteristics of the levels or grades in a grade and pay structure into which jobs will be placed. The grade definitions may refer to such job characteristics as skill, decision making and responsibility but these are not analysed separately. Evaluation takes place through a process of non-analytical matching or 'job slotting'. This involves comparing a 'whole' job description, ie one not analysed into factors, with the grade definitions to establish the grade with which the job most closely corresponds. The difference between non-analytical matching and job-to-grade analytical matching as described above is that in the latter case, the grade profiles are defined in terms of job evaluation factors, and analytically defined role profiles are matched with them factor by factor. However, the distinction between analytical and non-analytical matching can be blurred when the comparison is made between formal job descriptions and role profiles which have been prepared in a standard format that includes common headings for such aspects of jobs as levels of responsibility or knowledge and skill requirements. These 'factors' may not be compared specifically but will be taken into account when forming a judgement. But this may not satisfy the UK legal requirement that a scheme must be analytical to provide a defence in an equal pay claim.

Developing a matching scheme

The steps required to develop a matching scheme are set out below.

Step 1: Decide on type of scheme

The following decisions have to be made on the type of matching scheme:

(a) *Should it be analytical or non-analytical?* Conceptually, because jobs are analysed and compared in greater detail across a number of headings an analytical scheme will produce more accurate results. And it can be used to defend an equal pay claim. But non-analytical schemes are less trouble to develop and use and reasonably accurate results can be obtained if care is taken over the definition of job and grade profiles, by, for example, providing for them to be drawn up in a standard and readily comparable format.

(b) *Job-to-grade or job-to-job or both?* The framework provided by a defined grade structure (analytical or non-analytical) will help to make grading decisions that are consistent and defensible. The definition of a grade structure can have other uses, for example in organization design and development and career planning. The sole use of job-to-job matching allows for more flexibility in association with a spot rate pay structure (one without grades) and it may be easier to respond to market rate pressures. Adding job-to-job comparisons to job-to-grade comparisons can increase the accuracy of evaluations and, where benchmark jobs have been assigned to a grade, they provide examples that illustrate the characteristics of the grade and thus serve to reinforce judgements. Job-to-grade matching is frequently adopted as the basic approach in conjunction with job-to-job matching.

(c) *Use of a point-factor evaluation system.* Matching based on written role and grade profiles can be carried out without the use of a point-factor scheme. But such a scheme has three possible uses that can increase the accuracy of evaluations. First, it can provide definitions of the factors to be used in matching; second, it can be used to allocate benchmark jobs to grades; and third, it can reinforce evaluations by defining grades or benchmark jobs in points terms so that if required (for new jobs or ones which have been difficult to match in the usual way) a conventional points evaluation can be made. A combined development will start with the point-factor evaluation of benchmark jobs and the allocation of points ranges to grades but matching jobs to grade profiles will be the main form of evaluation.

Step 2: Prepare benchmark job profiles

A representative cross-section of jobs covering different levels and functions is selected at this stage. The number of jobs required varies according to the size and complexity of the organization. Even in a simple structure it will be 10 per cent or more and it could be much higher in some complex organizations (30 per cent or more). In a small organization this stage may involve preparing profiles for all jobs, rather than a benchmark sample. A typical profile will incorporate basic information about the job – the title, to whom the job holder is responsible and who is responsible to the job holder, the overall purpose of the job and a list of the key activities carried out (the key result areas).

An analytical job profile as shown in Table 8.1 also summarizes the characteristics of the job against a set of factor headings. If an existing point-factor scheme is being used as the basis for the evaluation, the factors contained in that scheme will be adopted. If not, a decision will need to be made on what factors are appropriate. The factors used in the job profile will be the same as those used to define grades in Step 3. Guidance on selecting factors is given in Chapter 5.

Job profiles may focus on an analysis of the key characteristics of the job without going into the other details, as is illustrated in Table 8.2.

Step 3: Design grade structure

If job-to-grade matching is to take place it is necessary to design a grade structure. This may have already been done following the initial benchmarking exercise when developing a point-factor scheme. If not, decisions on the structure have to be made. These will initially determine whether the structure should be a single one covering all jobs, or whether it should be a job family structure with differently defined structures for clusters of jobs with common characteristics. A decision will also have to be made on the provisional number of grades or levels (this number may be amended when the grade definition process takes place). This can be done at the outset based on an *a priori* view that is made empirically by reference to the existing hierarchy or a belief that the present number of grades should be reduced to a more manageable number. A less judgemental approach is to base the decision on a ranking of benchmark posts, possibly using paired comparisons, and an analysis of the clustering of jobs based on the identification of common characteristics. The ranked jobs are then divided into grades according to views on the number of the distinct levels of responsibility that exist in the organization.

Another approach is to get a project team to sort benchmark job descriptions, role profiles or questionnaire responses into levels, with the criteria for allocating jobs to different levels being discussed as part of the process. The outcomes from the discussion and the number of levels arrived at through the process can be built into the matching definitions, while information about which jobs fell into each level can be discarded pending a more thorough matching process.

Table 8.1   Example of a job profile

Job title	Call Centre Team Leader
Responsible to	Call Centre Manager
Responsible to job holder	Twelve call centre agents
Overall purpose of job	To control the efforts of a team of call centre agents to ensure they meet required standards
Key activities	• Monitor performance of complete team and each of its members against standard criteria, ie 80 per cent of calls to be answered within 20 seconds, average talk time no more than two minutes, no more than 3 per cent of customers hang up
	• Select agents
	• Train new agents
	• Encourage and guide agents who are not meeting targets
	• Invoke capability procedure if an agent persistently fails to achieve targets
	• Conduct regular team meetings to discuss performance issues and agree how performance could be improved
	Knowledge and skills (general)	• Knowledge of products on offer and company procedures
		• Knowledge of factors affecting the performance of agents and what can be done to improve their performance
	Interpersonal skills	• A high level of leadership, motivational and training skills required
		• Teambuilding skills
Factor analysis		• Ability to deal sensitively with performance problems
	Judgement and decision making	• Exercises own judgement on how to deal with people and performance issues in team although can request advice from HR business partner
	Complexity	• The work pattern does not vary much
	Responsibility for resources	• Leads a team of 12 people

Table 8.2 Example of a job profile for a higher education lecturer

1 Teaching and learning support	• Plan, design and deliver a number of modules within subject area. • Deliver at undergraduate and/or postgraduate levels across a range of modules. • Use appropriate teaching, learning support and assessment methods. • Supervise projects, field trips and, where appropriate, placements. • Supervise postgraduate students. • Identify areas where current course provision is in need of revision or improvement. • Contribute to the planning, design and development of course objectives and material. • Ensure in conjunction with colleagues that modules complement other courses taken by students. • Set, mark and assess coursework and examinations and provide feedback to students.
2 Research and scholarship	• Develop research objectives and proposals, obtain funding and design research projects. • Conduct individual and collaborative research projects, lead small research teams or play a major part in research teams. • Identify sources of funding and contribute to the process of securing funds. • Extend, transform and apply knowledge acquired through scholarly activities. • Write and referee journal articles, or write or contribute to textbooks and make presentations at national and international conferences.
3 Communication	• Communicate straightforward through to complex information to a variety of audiences, including students, peers and external contacts. • Use high-level presentation skills and a range of media.
4 Liaison and networking	• Liaise with colleagues in other departments and/or institutions on professional matters. • Participate in departmental and other committee meetings. • Join external networks to foster collaboration and share information and ideas. • May represent the department at external meetings.

(continued)

Table 8.2 *(Continued)*

5 **Managing people**	● Lead the delivery of teaching in a module or programme: plan the timetable, allocate teaching responsibilities, and monitor the delivery of programmes to ensure that they achieve learning objectives and are meeting quality standards. ● Lead small research teams. ● Act as mentor to more junior lecturers. ● Appraise staff and advise them on their personal development.
6 **Teamwork**	● Attend and actively participate in regular team meetings at which course development and delivery issues are discussed. ● Collaborate with colleagues to identify and respond to students' needs.
7 **Pastoral care**	● Use listening, interpersonal and pastoral care skills to deal with sensitive issues concerning students and provide support. ● Refer students as appropriate to services providing further help. ● Act as personal tutor.
8 **Initiative, problem solving and decision making**	● Identify the need for developing the content or structure of a course and put proposals together in conjunction with colleagues on how this should be achieved. ● Develop creative ideas as a result of research and scholarship. ● Deal with admission queries and problems concerning student performance. ● Sole responsibility to decide how to deliver own modules and assess students.
9 **Planning and managing resources**	● As module leader or tutor, liaise with colleagues on content and method of delivery. ● May plan and implement consultancy projects to generate income for the institution.
10 **Emotional demands**	● Work under pressure to deliver results.
11 **Work environment**	● Work in a stable environment or a laboratory or workshop.

(continued)

Table 8.2 *(Continued)*

12 Expertise	<ul><li>Possess in-depth knowledge of the subject.</li><li>Possess the required levels of expertise in teaching and research.</li><li>Update skills and knowledge continuously.</li><li>Understand equal opportunity issues as they impact upon the delivery of teaching and collegiate working.</li></ul>

Whichever approach is used, the number of levels may be amended at a later stage if it is shown to be inappropriate.

Analytical matching grade profiles

In an analytical matching scheme both grades and jobs are defined in terms of the selected set of factors or elements. These can be chosen specifically for the scheme using the methods suggested in Chapter 7, or the matching criteria could reproduce the factors in a point-factor scheme (one that already exists or one developed specially to back up matching). It may be desirable to combine sub-factors or any factors that are highly correlated (eg freedom to act and decision making). The degree to which matching is analytical will depend on the extent to which the elements represent discrete job dimensions (and then whether jobs are analysed separately according to each of these dimensions).

Where there is no pre-existing point-factor or analytical proprietary scheme the grade or level profiles will need to be developed from scratch. The easiest way to produce definitions is simply to draw up the grade profiles on the basis of assumptions about the characteristics of any jobs that would be placed in the various levels. An alternative approach is to select benchmark jobs covering all levels, analyse and rank them, allocate them to grades on a judgemental (felt-fair) basis and then prepare grade profiles by reference to the analyses of the benchmark jobs. However, where there is a pre-existing point-factor or analytical proprietary scheme the most robust method is to refer to the analyses of benchmark jobs that have already been graded and distil these to produce a generic definition. This is done by reviewing the job evaluation scores for each grade and creating a description for each level that reflects the typical pattern of responses for that grade.

Grade profiles can also indicate career paths. For this reason, at Friends Provident Insurance they are called career bands, as shown in Table 8.3.

Grade definitions or profiles can be specifically linked to a point-factor scheme as illustrated in Table 8.4.

An example of a more comprehensive framework produced for a large charity is shown in Table 8.5.

Separate grade profiles may be defined for each job family (groups of jobs with common characteristics) in job family structures. An example is given in Table 8.6. The definitions of knowledge and competency requirements at each level define the career path in this job family.

Non-analytical matching scheme grade profiles

Non-analytical matching grade profiles may be limited to a simple sentence describing the work done, such as 'carries out routine support or administrative services'. But as shown in Table 8.7, grade profiles may include common elements and thereby become semi-analytical. In such cases, the job profiles would have to cover each of the elements.

Step 4: Develop matching procedure

Matching will be job profile to grade profile or job profile to benchmark profile or both. It is necessary to decide who does the matching, how they should do it and the documentation to be made available.

Matching is usually carried out by a matching panel. This may be a group of line managers facilitated by HR, but it should preferably include employee representatives. Guidelines are required on matching. These may define a perfect profile match as one in which all the elements in the job profile match all the elements in the grade or benchmark role profile. In the event of the failure to attain a perfect match the guidelines may indicate:

- the number of matches required of individual elements to indicate that an acceptable profile match has been achieved, for example

Table 8.3 Friends Provident career band profiles

Career band A	Job example: clerical and administrative staff
Technical knowledge/business experience and qualifications	Developing a knowledge of one or more key areas within the function or business unit, together with an understanding of the systems utilized. Ensures that technical information is appropriately presented and correct.
Problem solving	Solves problems by following well-defined procedures and precedents. Will consult with more experienced colleagues on more difficult or novel situations.
Leadership	Takes responsibility for management of own workload, delivering against performance standards and individual/team objectives.
Communication/influence	Communicates information clearly and concisely, applying standards of common courtesy to all contacts.

Career band B	Job example: customer services consultant
Technical knowledge/business experience and qualifications	Demonstrates a good understanding of a range of non-standard processes, procedures and systems to be utilized in carrying out responsibilities. Is likely to have two or more years' relevant experience working within the function or business unit or to have gained relevant experience elsewhere. May be starting to study for specific technical exams, eg FPC or ACII.
Problem solving	Works within procedures and precedents determining solutions from a number of appropriate alternatives.
Leadership	Offers guidance and technical support to less experienced members of the team.
Communication/influence	Applies developed communication skills in effectively handling more challenging contacts.

(continued)

Table 8.3 *(Continued)*

Career band C	Job example: customer services team leader
Technical knowledge/business experience and qualifications	Fully conversant with the procedures, policies and systems applied within the function or business unit, having gained relevant experience over a period of five or more years. Demonstrates a comprehensive understanding of one or more well-defined areas for which they will provide technical leadership. Is developing an understanding of the relationship between different subject areas/business units. Is likely to have gained a qualification in a technical subject in a relevant discipline.
Problem solving	Applies specialist knowledge of own area in making judgements based on the analysis of factual information in straightforward situations.
Leadership	Plans and co-ordinates the work of the team and/or provides technical leadership, eg through delivery of on-the-job training, quality audits or application of developed specialist skills and knowledge.
Communication/influence	Explains technical information clearly and effectively, adopting a style of communication to fit differing levels of audience understanding. Is able to persuade colleagues and gain commitment to new ideas or approaches by expressing own views confidently and logically.

Career band D	Job examples: customer services team manager, analyst, programmer
Technical knowledge/business experience and qualifications	Is able to apply and consolidate specialist skills and knowledge gained over a period of eight or more years' relevant experience to ensure essential procedures are followed and standards maintained. Demonstrates an understanding of the relationship between different subject areas and applies this knowledge in delivering cross-functional support, projects or advice.
	As a professional entrant to the business, will be developing professional skills through exam success and be increasing their contribution to the business.
Problem solving	Uses analytical skills and evaluative judgment, based on the analysis of factual and qualitative information to solve problems of a non-routine or more complex nature. Will be guided by precedents.
Leadership	In a team management role will be handling staff management issues including recruitment, resource management, training, coaching and performance management, and playing a leading role in determining salary recommendations for team members. Alternatively, will be a technical specialist with well-developed technical skills and specialist knowledge.
Communication/influence	Demonstrates strong verbal and written communication skills in influencing the outcome of decisions. Involves appropriate contacts in developing the final solution.

Table 8.4 Grade definitions based on a point-factor scheme

Level	Definition
1	• The use of the skills required to carry out straightforward work.
	• Requires the skills to work well with others and respond politely and competently to requests and enquiries.
	• The work is well defined and relatively few new situations are encountered. The causes of problems are readily identifiable and can be dealt with easily.
	• Work requirements involve a fairly limited range of activities.
	• Responsible only for the equipment required to carry out the work.
2	• The application of specific administrative or technical skills.
	• Requires the skills to exert some influence over others, getting them to accept a proposal or point of view.
	• Evaluation of information is required to deal with occasional new problems and situations and to decide on a course of action from known alternatives. Specific guidelines exist on what needs to be done and the more complex problems are referred to a higher authority.
	• There is some diversity in the work, which involves a number of non-routine elements and the exercise of a variety of skills although they are quite closely related to one another.
	• May have two or three staff reporting to him or her, and/or monitors expenditure.
3	• The application of a range of professional, specialist, technical, administrative or operational areas of knowledge and skills.
	• Requires the skills frequently to relate to people inside and outside the organization, providing advice and guidance, dealing with problems affecting people and exerting influence on important matters. The skills may be used in negotiations and joint problem solving on relatively straightforward issues.
	• Exercises discriminating judgement in dealing with relatively new or unusual problems where a wide range of information has to be considered and the courses of action are not immediately obvious. Takes independent action within defined policy frameworks.
	• The work is diverse, consisting of a number of different elements, which are only broadly related to one another, and the exercise of a wide variety of skills.
	• May lead a small team, and/or manage a small budget or be responsible for a range of facilities or equipment.

(continued)

Table 8.4 *(Continued)*

Level	Definition
4	• The application of high levels of professional, specialist, technical or administrative expertise. • Requires the skills constantly to relate to people at senior levels inside and outside the organization on non-routine issues, providing advice and guidance internally on the interpretation and application of company policies. • Frequently exercises independent judgement when faced with unusual problems and situations where no policy guidelines or precedents are available. • The work is highly diverse, involving many different elements, which may not be closely related to one another. • Leads a large team or department of more than 10 people, and/ or acts as budget manager for a department or office.
5	• The application of authoritative expertise in a key area of the organization's activities. • Requires the skills to deal with internal and external contacts at high levels, handling important and non-routine issues and involving the exercise of considerable persuasive ability, sensitivity to others and tact. The skills may be used when conducting important negotiations, dealing with difficult and sensitive cases or acting as the recognized representative of the company on key issues externally. • Deals on own initiative with widely differing problems calling for extreme clarity of thought in assessing conflicting information and balancing the risks associated with possible solutions. • The work is multidisciplinary and involves making a broad range of highly diverse decisions. • Leads a major function or range of activities and manages a commensurately sized budget.

Table 8.5 (a) Grade profiles

Factor	Grade 1	Grade 2	Grade 3
Supervisory responsibility	Little or no supervisory responsibility other than helping/inducting less experienced staff in the work of the group.	Minor supervisory responsibility, eg in the absence of Section Head allocation of work and checking for quality and quantity.	Occasional supervision of staff temporarily assigned or shared supervision of permanent staff.
Creativity	Work with very limited opportunity for creative work or innovatory thinking.	Work largely regulated by laid down procedures, but needing occasional creative skills.	Creativity is a feature of the job but exercised within the general framework of recognized procedures.
Contacts	Contacts and exchanges information within the organization beyond the immediate associates, but usually within the post's own department. Exchange usually on non-contentious and well-established matters.	Contacts with employees of other departments or occasionally receiving enquiries from outside the authority as first contact. Contacts beyond the organization's employees would be within limited terms of reference and generally be restricted to situations where information is readily available.	Contacts which are generally not contentious but where the need or potential outcome may not be straightforward, or where the circumstances call for an element of tact or sensitivity. Contacts at this level would include interviewing to establish details or service needs, the supply of straightforward advice and initiating action to provide assistance. Contacts within the organization would require the provision of advice or guidance on matters which are less well established.

Decisions	Post requires little freedom to act, work is carried out within clearly defined rules or procedures and advice is available if required. Decisions have limited and short-term effect on employees beyond immediate colleagues or on the public. Effects of decisions would be quickly known and readily amended if necessary.	Work is carried out within clearly defined rules and procedures involving decisions chosen from a range of established alternatives. Decisions have an effect on the internal operations of the post's own or other departments or on the individual or on the provision of service to the public.	Work is carried out within policies and objectives where there is a wide range of choices and where advice is not normally available. AND/OR Decisions where policy, procedures and working standards provide only general guidelines. Decisions which have significant implications for the organization or significant effects on employees or other individuals or other organizations.
Knowledge and skills	Ability to undertake work, consistent with a basic knowledge and skills requirement, which involves a limited range of tasks that can be carried out after initial induction.	Ability to undertake work, consistent with a comparatively basic knowledge and skills requirement, which encompasses a range of tasks involving application of readily understood rules.	Ability to undertake work concerning one more involved tasks confined to one function or area of activity which requires a good standard or practical knowledge and skills in that area of activity.
Work context	Work where the programme of tasks is not normally interrupted.	Work subject to interruption to programme of tasks but not involving any significant change to the programme.	Work subject to changing problems or circumstances or demand.

(continued)

Table 8.5 (b) Grade profiles (*Continued*)

Factor	Grade 4	Grade 5	Grade 8
Supervisory responsibility	Supervision of staff carrying out tasks in one identifiable area of work.	Supervision or co-ordination and planning of the work of groups of staff carrying out work of a diverse nature.	Plan and organize a large department or highly significant area of activity and/or manage a portfolio of important short- and long-term projects to meet both internal and external requirements.
Creativity	Creativity is essential to the job and needs to be regularly exercised within general guidelines.	Work which requires creative input in a number of diverse subjects and range of expertise where the frequent opportunity and need for imaginative thinking is not limited by defined policies.	Carry out work in unprecedented situations frequently involving innovatory response on diverse subjects, which have extensive policy or service implications. Make a major contribution to high-profile reviews of key organization policies.
Contacts	Contacts which deal with situations where the content and outcome are not straightforward. Contacts within the authority with staff on matters which are not well-established and where some authority in the provision of services is required.	Contacts regularly dealing with a range of complex and contentious matters where the outcome will have substantial implications for the contact or the organization's service provision. Though the post operates within broad policy guidelines, the handling of contacts would demand a consistently high degree of discretion, sensitivity and advocacy.	Contacts advising the organization on high-level complex matters with profound implications for the person or the organization contacted or which require a responsibility to act on behalf of the organization and commit the organization to a course of action involving substantial impact on resources. It would be expected that the expert guidance would be accepted and only ever overruled as a result of a change in policies.

Decisions	Decisions which lead to the setting of working standards in the provision of operational services or changes in important procedures or service practice.	Decisions involve independent action within precise policy frameworks.	Decisions made within broad policy frameworks, which have a profound impact on the organization's policies and activities across a number of departments or on large numbers of people or on organizations in receipt of the organization's services.
Knowledge and skills	Ability to undertake work on a variety of advanced tasks confined to one function or area of activity which requires detailed knowledge and skills in a specialist discipline.	Undertake work of a highly complex and diverse nature which requires advanced/high-level knowledge and skills in a range of specialist disciplines.	Possess highly developed specialist knowledge across a range of work procedures and practices underpinned by theoretical knowledge and relevant practical experience.
Work context	Work subject to frequently changing circumstances	Work is highly complex and frequently involves the resolution of conflicting priorities.	Work demands are largely unpredictable; may be involved in crisis management on issues deeply affecting the organization.

Table 8.6 Job family level profiles

Level	Role	Key responsibilities	Key competencies
8	HR Director	• Contribute to development of business strategy • Develop HR strategies aligned to business strategy • Exercise overall direction of all HR activities required to support achievement of business goals • Oversee human capital management projects	Knowledge of: • the business, its strategy and its drivers • HRM/HCM at a strategic level Ability to: • articulate a vision and set a leadership agenda • contribute to business strategic planning on equal terms with other directors • develop and implement HR strategies which are aligned to the business strategy and integrated with one another
5	Learning and Development Manager	• Contribute to the development of the learning and development strategy • Identify learning needs and plan blended learning and development programmes to meet them • Deliver major programmes • Direct the activities of learning and development consultants	Knowledge of: • current thinking and good practice in learning and development • advanced concepts and techniques in the field (Fellow CIPD) Ability to: • analyse key factors affecting activities in the function • coordinate and direct complex HRD programmes

		Knowledge of:
4	Assistant Head of Talent Management	• Contribute to the preparation of human capital plans • Assist in preparing management succession plans • Coordinate performance management activities • Analyse human capital data and prepare reports	• techniques of human resource and management succession planning • HRM at the level of Member, CIPD with at least eight years' experience Ability to: • analyse business plans and draw conclusions on talent management requirements • carry out the analysis and diagnosis of people issues and propose practical solutions
3	HR Business Partner	• Contribute to the effective management of the division • Ensure the division has the skilled people it requires • Work alongside line managers and provide help and advice on HR issues • Deliver HR services required by the division	Knowledge of: • HRM techniques at the level of Member, CIPD with at least four years' experience • business imperatives in the division • corporate HR policies and practices Ability to: • provide efficient and cost-effective services in each HR area • promote the empowerment of line managers to make HR decisions but provide guidance as required. • anticipate requirements and set up and operate appropriate services

(continued)

Table 8.6 (Continued)

Level	Role	Key responsibilities	Key competencies
2	Reward Analyst	• Maintain information systems on pay and benefits • Assist in the conduct and analysis of market surveys • Maintain data bank of information on market rates • Prepare role profiles for job evaluation purposes	Knowledge of: • the labour market and sources of market data • reward management techniques at the level of the CIPD Certificate in Reward Management Ability to: • carry out numerical and statistical analysis • use IT systems, software and spreadsheets • conduct role analyses
1	HR Assistant (recruitment)	• Place job advertisements • Arrange interviews • Deal with routine correspondence to applicants including standard offer letters • Ensure records created for new employees	Knowledge of: • HR techniques relevant to recruitment (studying for CIPD) Ability to: • select appropriate media • administer fairly complex procedures
1	Administrative Assistant	• Provide word processing services • Maintain records • Operate office machinery • Deal with routine queries	Knowledge of: • Microsoft Office – Word, Excel, PowerPoint Ability to: • word process all types of documents, including reports and complex tabulations • prepare PowerPoint presentations • administer standard procedures

Table 8.7 A semi-analytical grade profile framework

Grade	Grade profiles
A	Provide basic administrative and support services. Work largely prescribed.
B	Provide fairly complex administrative and support services. Work is largely standardized but there is some freedom to decide on methods and priorities.
C	Provide complex administrative and support services or technical support. There is some diversity in role requirements but acts within specific and detailed policy and procedural guidelines.
D	Manage certain operations within a function or provide professional services in a key area. The work is diverse – act within broad policy guidelines.
E	Manage a function or department within an operational or technical area or is the main provider of professional advice and services in a key aspect of the organization's activities. The work is highly diverse there is freedom to act within broad policy frameworks.
F	Operational head of a major department, making a major impact on the performance of the organization. The work is complex and involves making a broad range of highly diverse decisions. A considerable amount of independent action is required within the framework of the organization's strategies and plans and subject only to general guidance.
G	Involved in creating a shared vision and mission and strategic goals for the organization as a member of the board. Formulate strategies for a key function and ensure that functional strategies are implemented to achieve strategic goals.

five out of six; it is usual to restrict the mismatches allowed to fairly small variations – if there are any large ones, the match would be invalidated;

- any elements which *must* match for there to be a profile match, for example it may be decided that there must be a match for an element covering knowledge and skills;

- the procedure for grading if there has been a mismatch; this may require further information about the job or a full evaluation of the role if the matching process is underpinned by a point-factor scheme.

Step 5: Test the matching procedure

In a large job evaluation project where there are a number of panels it is advisable to test the grade profiles and the matching protocol by preparing a representative set of individual role profiles or questionnaire responses using the same format of factors and then matching the latter to the former. Any difficulties in doing this and achieving a sensible result, or any problems with the matching rules, will indicate what changes need to be made to the grade profiles.

Step 6: Train matching panel

The panel should be trained in the matching process and the use of the guidelines or protocols using real examples. It is essential to carry out this training thoroughly as the process is likely to be completely unfamiliar to the panel members, except in a small organization where the project team may have been involved throughout the development process. Training is needed even where the scheme is non-analytical and the matching process is on a whole job basis, as panel members will still need to be reminded about basic principles of job evaluation, including the need to match the job not the person, and how to avoid potential bias.

Step 7: Conduct matching

The panel conducts matching in accordance with the guidelines. If matching cannot be agreed the panel may request further information or refer the job to be evaluated by the basic job evaluation scheme, where matching is underpinned by a factor plan.

Examples

Syngenta

Syngenta is involved in agribusiness – the research, development, manufacture and sale of agrochemicals, seeds, plants and lawn-care products. It has around 2,000 employees in the UK.

Syngenta was formed in 2000 from a merger of the agribusiness interests of AstraZeneca and Novartis. The company wanted to move away from its existing points-based job evaluation arrangements and try to bring together the inconsistent pay structures across the business areas in the UK. It also wanted an approach to job evaluation and pay that would operate across the UK and fit the culture of the newly merged company.

A new job grading and linked pay structure was introduced consisting of six broad bands or work levels, covering everyone in the UK except for the most senior leaders and some workers in the manufacturing environment. This replaced a 15-grade structure.

The company previously used Hay, but did not wish to continue with the laborious and analytical processes involved in writing job descriptions to a particular format, preparing cases and getting senior managers together to review them. The complexity of the Hay system meant that managers needed technical job evaluation skills to manage the system rather than applying their knowledge and understanding of the roles and discussing their content and impact. The mathematical nature of the system also led to little ownership of the outcomes of the job evaluation system. More often than not, they were seen to be the results of a mysterious process carried out behind closed doors. In addition, even a points-based system requires judgement and interpretation, so it was decided that a less analytical and mathematical system would reduce the unproductive time spent on process and need not undermine the robustness of the final outcomes. Under the previous system it was easy for people to spend fruitless time working out how they could get additional points in order to reach a higher grade.

Syngenta wanted the new arrangements to be owned by line managers. There was a desire to use managers' knowledge about the roles in their functional areas to best effect in a simple, line-owned grading structure. The system was therefore designed to encourage line managers to contribute to grading decisions and to set both pay benchmarks and individual salaries. To underpin this, the new arrangements were 'co-created' with senior managers and owned by them.

Job matching

There are six work levels, populated with a number of generic role profiles. The levels are defined by a number of factors, the most significant of which is the degree of responsibility and autonomy. The role descriptions vary in each of four business areas: research and development, manufacturing, marketing and sales, and business support. Most business activities (such as HR) have job families – a ladder of generic roles. This provides clarity for leaders and employees on potential career paths available, and supports the allocation of new roles into existing ladders. In the science area, for example, there are 10 different generic roles spread over several work levels, each of which is benchmarked against the market. In order to manage career progression and recognize growth in role size and contribution, there are often two benchmarks within a work level.

There is no direct linkage between work levels and salaries, although the on-target annual bonus increases by work level, and work level six roles typically receive a car allowance to reflect the external market.

Process

There are three local job-sizing panels – one for research and development, one for UK manufacturing, and one for commercial and support staff. In addition, there is a UK job-sizing panel, which takes an overview for consistency between the different parts of the business. The UK manufacturing panel, for example, consists of the head of UK manufacturing, the site managers for the two manufacturing sites, the head of HR and the head of UK engineering. The UK job-sizing panel consists of the site heads and other senior managers, including some from outside the UK. HR managers are members of panels alongside other managers, but their role is no different to that of the other managers. The function of the panel is to question, challenge and fully understand any rationale for a change of work level or benchmark. The company recognizes that it is important to have people on the panel with the credibility and confidence to challenge their colleagues, even in different functional areas where they may have less expert knowledge.

The panels usually meet once a year and approve promotions, grade changes and changes to benchmarks. They also set the benchmarks for all the jobs for their area, following recommendations from managers and HR managers who have reviewed salary survey data. The company takes part in a number of surveys and benchmarks the ladders of generic roles. External data influences what Syngenta pays but does not directly determine it – management judgement and data in combination will determine the final benchmark changes. Syngenta wishes to pay competitively in the markets in which it competes for talent. In practice, this means that benchmarks are often set at the median of market data. Actual pay is generally between 80 per cent and 120 per cent of the benchmark, and is very largely based on performance.

Involving first line managers

HR worked with senior managers to design and implement the new structures but it is necessary to build and develop for all leaders their knowledge of and comfort with the job evaluation and benchmarking systems. The HR team is now trying to provide more support to first line managers when they are having pay-related discussions with their employees. Information on the background to the salary budget, the link to total pay, and how salary benchmarks are set needs to be shared more openly and employees and leaders need to feel confident to engage in conversations around this often difficult and uncomfortable area. Syngenta is therefore trying to provide opportunities for first line managers to discuss pay-related matters with senior leaders so that they have the opportunity to ask whatever questions they need in order to deepen their understanding.

Advice

Syngenta is satisfied with its job evaluation arrangements, which it describes as 'a good balance between robustness and pragmatism, ensuring that grading is robust and consistent but that the time spent on it is focused on discussing and comparing role content and impact rather than mathematical points allocation'. It advises others introducing job evaluation systems to look for opportunities to involve line managers in role-sizing discussions and to ensure that managers feel ownership of the process. It advises against having a system policed by HR, or which HR are implementing because 'they know best'. It is very easy to turn job evaluation into a mathematical process that underutilizes the understanding and knowledge of managers in the business, and makes role sizing a purely theoretical and analytical process. Resisting this temptation and balancing analysis with knowledge and judgement has proved a far better approach for Syngenta.

The NHS job evaluation scheme

The NHS job evaluation scheme was first developed to support the programme for modernizing the NHS pay system, called 'Agenda for Change'. With some modifications it is now used to grade jobs throughout the NHS. Essentially, the scheme uses analytical matching but it is underpinned by a bespoke point-factor scheme.

Development stages

The stages in developing the NHS job evaluation scheme, which were overseen by a joint management/trade union job evaluation working party (the JEWP), were:

1 Identify draft factors by reference to schemes already in use in the NHS.

2 Test draft factors. This was done using a sample of around 100 jobs. Volunteer job holders were asked to complete an open-ended questionnaire, providing information under each of the draft factor headings and any other information about their jobs, which they felt was not covered by the draft factors. The draft factors were then refined.

3 Develop factor levels. The information collected during the initial test exercise was used by small joint teams to identify and define draft levels of demand for each factor.

4 Test draft factor plan. A benchmark sample of around 200 jobs was drawn up, with two or three individuals being selected for each job to complete a more specific factor-based questionnaire, helped by trained job analysts, to ensure that the information provided was accurate and comprehensive.

5 Evaluate completed questionnaires – this was done by trained joint panels. The outcomes were reviewed by JEWP members and the validated results were then put on a computer database.

6 Decide scoring and weighting. The job evaluation results database was used to test various scoring and weighting options for

consideration by the JEWP and the JSG (the Joint Secretaries Group).

7 Produce provisional guidance notes on how to apply the factor level definitions to jobs consistently. These were then expanded as a result of the benchmark evaluation exercise and have continued to be developed following successive training and profiling.

8 Computerize. The scale of implementing the NHS job evaluation JE scheme meant it was essential to consider how it could be computerized. A bespoke computerized JE software package was developed to assist in the process of matching and evaluating local jobs under the rules of the scheme.

The main features of the scheme are described below.

The factor plan

Table 8.8 The factor plan

	Levels							
Factor	**1**	**2**	**3**	**4**	**5**	**6**	**7**	**8**
1 Communication and relationship skills	5	12	21	32	45	80		
2 Knowledge, training and experience	18	38	80	88	120	158	198	240
3 Analytical skills	8	15	27	42	80			
4 Planning and organization skills	8	15	27	42	80			
5 Physical skills	8	15	27	42	80			
6 Responsibility – patient/client care	4	9	15	22	30	39	49	80
7 Responsibility – policy and service	5	12	21	32	45	80		
8 Responsibility – finance and physical	5	12	21	32	45	80		
9 Responsibility – staff/HR/leadership/ training	5	12	21	32	45	80		

(continued)

Table 8.8   *(Continued)*

Factor		Levels						
	1	**2**	**3**	**4**	**5**	**6**	**7**	**8**
10 Responsibility – information resources	4	9	18	24	34	48	80	
11 Responsibility – research and development	5	12	21	32	45	80		
12 Freedom to act	5	12	21	32	45	80		
13 Physical effort	3	7	12	18	25			
14 Mental effort	3	7	12	18	25			
15 Emotional effort	5	11	18	25				
16 Working conditions	3	7	12	18	25			

The model has a maximum of 1,000 points available. The number of points available for each factor is distributed between the levels on an increasing whole number basis. Groups of similar factors should have equal weights but because the NHS is a knowledge-based organization, a higher weighting to knowledge was justified. It was considered that differentiation worked best when scores were stretched and this was achieved through a non-linear approach to scoring.

Profiles

Profiles for benchmark jobs were developed in order to make the processes of assigning staff to a pay band as straightforward as possible. The matching procedure allows most jobs locally to be matched to nationally evaluated profiles, on the basis of information from job descriptions, person specifications and oral information.

The matching process

The matching process is based primarily on agreed and up-to-date job descriptions for the jobs to be considered. The matching is carried out by panels. Their function is to:

- identify possible profile matches (there are unlikely to be more than three possible matches);

- compare the profile job statements with the job description, person specification and any other available information, including that provided orally by job group advisers/representatives, for the job to be matched;
- on a factor-by-factor basis, compare the information on the job with that in the selected profile and determine the extent to which they match.

A perfect match is achieved if all factor levels are within the range specified on the profile. If most factor levels match, but there are a small number of variations, there may still be a match so long as all the following conditions apply: (1) the variations are of not more than one level above or below; (2) the variations do not relate to the knowledge or freedom to act factors (3) the variations do not apply to more than five factors; and (4) the score variations do not take the job over a grade boundary. If there is no match the process is repeated with another profile. If there is no other possible profile, the job is referred for local evaluation.

Matching in universities

The matching approach to job evaluation has been adopted by a number of British universities. At Birmingham, Imperial College, Southampton and other universities the method involves the development of job families. This is done by means of the Hay Group job family modelling technique. As defined by Hay, a job family describes a number of different roles which are engaged in similar work, and a job family model considers how many levels of that type of work there are and defines them in a way that clearly differentiates the levels. Jobs are evaluated by slotting them into the level in their job family that provides the closest match. A position has to match a level description by at least 80 per cent to be slotted into a level.

The matching process is underpinned by the Hay Guide Chart system of job evaluation. If a good match cannot be obtained, the Hay system is used to evaluate the job. Below is an example of a level descriptor used in Southampton University for level 3 posts in the Operational Services job family.

General

Roles at this level either manage operational services work of some volume or complexity or provide advice and technical input based on extensive practical learning. Dealing with people is an important ingredient, whether they are staff managed by the jobholder, contractors or customers, and there is often budgetary responsibility or impact.

Representative work activities

Managerial roles:

- establish and review work requirements taking account of customer needs, college policies and available resources;
- plan own and others' work for weeks and months ahead;
- implement plans for a service area ensuring effective operation;
- ensure staff are trained to required standards;
- monitor staff performance and take action to improve where needed;
- review customer satisfaction and, following discussion with more senior managers if appropriate, take steps to improve the service where necessary;
- review expenditure against budget, instigating corrective actions as necessary;
- ensure health and safety regulations are met.

Non-managerial roles:

- provide advice to colleagues and customers based on in-depth knowledge and technical expertise;
- analyse problems, diagnose and implement solutions, seeking agreement where appropriate;
- plan own work for weeks and months ahead;
- discuss and resolve problems or new requirements with customers, line managers and other colleagues;
- coach others to help them acquire skills and experience.

Either role type:

- contribute ideas for service improvement, changes to procedures and forward planning;
- discuss and resolve problems and concerns with customers and/or contractors;
- ensure that the service meets agreed needs.

Knowledge, skills and experience

- Vocational training plus practical experience, or the equivalent in practical experience;
- knowledge of college policies and processes;
- ability to solve a range of day-to-day problems without reference to others;
- skills in planning and organizing work and services;
- for managerial roles, ability to motivate staff, dealing with poor performance.

Performance criteria

Evidence of:

- quality and reliability of services provided/individual work, eg from customer feedback;
- effectiveness of planning and prioritizing;
- effective problem solving;
- customer satisfaction;
- flexibility;
- effectiveness in staff supervision, where appropriate;
- quality of contribution to the service and its development.

Levelling 09

'Levelling' is an approach to job evaluation that has come to the fore fairly recently although its roots are in more traditional forms of job evaluation and earlier attempts to define levels of responsibility. This chapter starts with a definition of levelling and a summary of these earlier approaches. It continues with a description of the 'DMA' system, which is based on the analysis of work levels.

Levelling defined

Levelling is a method of job evaluation that focuses on defining the levels of work in an organization and fitting jobs into those levels. It can simply be an alternative term for an analytical job-matching or job-classification scheme that allocates jobs into a hierarchy of grades by matching job definitions with the most relevant of the grade definitions. The difference is that in a proper levelling scheme the emphasis is on defining and describing how the organization is structured as a basis for considering the relative value of jobs, rather than on simply measuring relative worth. The work levels technique is concerned with the design of an organization, how work is structured in a hierarchy and the career paths available. It aims to fuse job evaluation with OD and talent management considerations. This can extend its purpose well beyond that of a traditional job evaluation programme.

As explained by Brown and Munday (2016):

Levelling is faster, more efficient and flexible than the ponderous points-factor systems of old, but still provides an objective, robust and effective foundation for fair and consistent pay setting and management. Points-factor evaluation may still be undertaken for difficult or controversial jobs, but most jobs are simply slotted into the appropriate level, and then the focus is on developing people's skills and contribution, which drives their pay progression up clearly communicated career pathways. Managers understand and accept banding decisions, while employees are engaged by the clarity and links between their pay progression and development of their skills and talents.

The notion of levelling as described above was first developed by Brian Dive in Unilever and Tesco in the 1990s. The methodology involved was called the 'DMA' (decision-making accountability) system. This system has been used by several large companies and levelling has since been adopted with enthusiasm by a number of consultancies.

Brown and Dive (2009) commented that, 'Organizations such as Unilever, Tesco and Vodafone are using such approaches to develop flatter, more flexible organization and job designs in which future leadership talent can flow and grow.'

Earlier approaches to levelling

As noted above, there is nothing new about evaluating jobs by defining levels of responsibility and fitting them into the most relevant level. And some time ago two people developed methodologies for doing so which, although they were little used in the UK, have influenced later developments. The people concerned were Elliott Jaques (1956) with his concept of the time span of discretion, and Thomas Paterson (1972) with his system of decision banding.

Jaques' time span of discretion

Research conducted by Elliott Jaques into payment methods at Glacier Metal in the UK led him to the conclusion that a time span could be calculated for a job by analysing the decisions that had to be taken. From this information could be discovered the maximum length of time for which the decisions made by a person on their own initiative committed resources of the company. Later analysis led to the finding that the higher the executive level the longer the time span and thus the conclusion was reached that the maximum time span of discretion could be used to measure the level of work. This was confirmed by an analysis of the levels of work in Glacier Metal and the time spans for jobs at each level classified as one hour, one day, one week, one to two years, two to five years, and over five years.

The following procedure was recommended by Jaques for assessing work levels in terms of time spans:

1 Tease out the discretionary content of the work allocated to a particular job.

2 Discover the mechanism used to review the use of discretion by someone doing the job.

3 Discover the maximum period of time that would elapse during which job holders were authorized and expected to exercise on their own account in discharging the responsibilities allocated to them.

This concept enabled Jaques to describe a 'requisite organization' as one in which each level in the hierarchy had its own distinctive time span.

The attraction of this theory is that it seems to provide one unique but universal factor as the basis for evaluation. It also provides a basis for analysing and reviewing organization structures. The notion of a time span of discretion attracted a lot of attention at the time and is still in use in some schemes as one factor amongst others measuring different levels of responsibility. However, although time span may be a factor that helps to indicate the level of work, the problem is one of measurement. In practice it is a nebulous concept and difficult to apply rigorously. It has been found that the assessment of time spans for other than fairly basic jobs becomes increasingly difficult at higher levels, which leads to approximations without any inherent validity. Moreover, the concept does not give a clear picture of the actual quality required in work and how it varies at each level. The use of time span as a sole criterion is therefore very rare.

Paterson's decision band method

Thomas Paterson, professor of engineering at the University of Strathclyde, stated that jobs have only one thing in common; they all require decisions to be made, and so they can be compared on the basis of the kinds and numbers of decisions. He distinguished six bands of decisions that, on the basis of his experience in engineering, he defined as follows.

Band E: Policy making – on the broad direction in which the firm is going, made by the board.

Band D: Programming – in planning how to carry out the policy, such as deciding on a master schedule of production.

Band C: Interpretive – in deciding, within the limits of the plan, what is to be done, for example, what the machine loading will be, how many persons to be allocated, what costing procedures are required.

Band B: Routine – on process, *how* to do what has been decided by an interpretative decision, for example the decision made by a skilled turner or by a senior clerk on how costs should be calculated.

Band A: Automatic – on the operations that go to make up a process, for example by a machinist who decides how to operate a lathe once it has been set up, or by a clerk who decides how to use the standard forms in calculating costs.

Band 0: Defined – on the elements that go to make up an operation, made by people who have already been taught precisely what their operations are and how to carry them out; the kind of decisions that can be learned in a very short time, from minutes up to a few days, for example by an operative on parts assembly or by a cleaner.

To recognize the fact that a job in one decision band may involve the coordination of jobs in the same band, each band with the exception of 0 can be divided into grades.

The merit of this approach is that a single well-defined factor is used which can be applied to all types of jobs. Decision making is an easy concept to grasp and is readily accepted as an important element in distinguishing between job levels. It is, however, essentially a job-classification scheme and suffers from the typical drawbacks of such methods, namely inflexibility and insensitivity. And the fact that it is non-analytical means that under UK equal pay law, the evaluations reached by this method cannot be used to defend an equal pay claim.

The decision-making accountability (DMA) approach

The DMA approach assumes that any organization has a genetic code of decision-making accountability and jobholders are held to account to ensure that it achieves its purpose. The complexity of accountability increases as people move up the organization. A decision is defined by Brian Dive (2004), who developed the method, as 'a considered act in response to a demand or need, to progress a process, change a state of affairs or solve a problem'. Accountability occurs when one is answerable to a higher authority for work, resources and results. Results could include service.

The approach was based on the empirical evidence provided by the extensive research led by Brian Dive undertaken globally over 10 years at Unilever and Tesco. He emphasized that, 'The key premise is that jobholders must take decisions that cannot be taken at a lower level and which need not be taken at a higher level.'

The appropriate accountability level for each job is established by assessing the following elements:

1 *Nature of work* – how it differs in essence from those below and above.

2 *Resource complexity*.

3 *Problem solving*.

4 *Change* – the accountability for driving change.

5 *Natural work team* – the accountability for lateral collaboration with peers.

6 *External interaction* – the accountability for external interaction with consumers, customers and suppliers.

7 *Timeframe* – the average time it takes to complete the balance of tasks for which a person is responsible.

DMA as a form of levelling was first applied by Unilever. It was used as the basis for replacing 17 job classes with five work levels that better structured reward and talent development processes. The DMA model has now spread across many different industries as well as the public and voluntary sectors.

Tesco used the DMA approach to move away from a point-factor job evaluation system and 22-grade structure towards a six-band structure of work levels. Work levels progress from level one, covering clerical and administrative jobs, up to board and senior directors in levels five and six. Jobs are allocated to a level according to the seven elements of accountability in the DMA model. The pay bands are relatively wide, with actual pay managed against market-related reference points set for about 100 benchmark roles based on the practices of 20 blue-chip companies. Work levels have also been applied to develop more effective organization design and reduce costs. In the Tesco structure, all staff must report to an individual in the work level above their own. These work levels underpin Tesco's group leadership development programme, linked to key competencies.

As reported by Brown and Dive (2009), other firms adopting the levelling approach include Vodafone and Novartis. Vodafone operates a system that uses eight global broad bands encompassing all jobs. Accountability descriptors exist for each band and roles are slotted into this framework. At the most senior levels and for the roles most difficult to slot, more detailed descriptors are used under headings such as business impact, leadership and innovation. The banding framework is mapped onto external databases for pay benchmarking and to support core reward processes such as incentives and benefits allocation.

Novartis uses a flat framework of bands to classify on a common basis the jobs of more than 90,000 employees in over 50 countries. A brief general description covers the types of job at each level, but then more detailed descriptions can be used to place jobs at the appropriate level in one of their functional specialist job families, which together constitute a global job family catalogue that essentially replaces traditional job evaluation. The firm's compensation policy makes no reference to internal fairness or job evaluation, instead explaining: 'Our compensation system offers competitive compensation that is aligned with industry practice and supports the realization of our vision and a performance-oriented culture that allows Novartis to reward people who perform well (and) be competitive with world-class companies and industry peers.' Pay ranges at each level vary by job family and location, supported by extensive market pay analysis.

References

Brown, D and Dive, B (2009) Level pegging, *People Management*, 15 January, pp 26–29

Brown, D and Munday, S (2016) *Stability rhymes with agility, pay structure needs to go with flexibility*, Opinion Paper 26, Institute for Employment Studies

Dive, B (2004) *The Healthy Organization*, London, Kogan Page

Jaques, E (1956) *Measurement of Responsibility*, Cambridge, MA, Harvard University Press

Paterson, T T (1972) *Job Evaluation: A new method*, London, Business Books

Market pricing 10

Market pricing is defined by the CIPD (2017) as 'a system of collecting data on the pay rates for similar jobs in other organizations to establish their market rate and track movements in those rates. The aim is to set the organization's own pay rates at an appropriate level to recruit and retain the staff it needs.' It is based on market rate analysis.

The CIPD also comments:

> Although the concept of a market rate for a job is common, there's no such thing as an accurate single rate of pay for a job or role, and rates may vary within the same occupation and in the same location. It's important for employers to consider carefully how to interpret the data collected and where the organization wants to position its salary and total remuneration levels in relation to the market.

It was reported by XpertHR (2012) that 95 per cent of respondents in the UK are now using market-linked pay comparisons in some form. A survey by WorldatWork in 2013 established that in the United States: 'Market pricing continues to well outpace all other methods as the dominant form of job evaluation with between 67 per cent and 73 per cent prevalence, depending on job category. Point factor is the second most prevalent method, but is well behind at 15 per cent to 18 per cent.'

Market pricing can be used generally in the design of graded pay structures. Specifically, it is used to determine the rates of pay for jobs in a spot rate or individual job range system. A spot rate is a rate for a job or an individual, which is not fitted into a grade or band in a conventional grade structure and does not allow any scope for pay progression. An individual job range is in effect a spot rate in which there is a defined range for pay progression. Market pricing can also provide the basis for fixing rates of pay in a broad-banded structure (see Chapter 11) and for informing the design of market groups in a job family structure (also see Chapter 11).

In this chapter consideration is given to:

- the two applications of market pricing;
- the case for market pricing;
- the process of market rate analysis;
- the limitations of market pricing.

Applications of market pricing

The term market pricing is used in two senses. First, it generally describes the process of analysing market rates to ensure that the rates of pay for individual jobs are competitive and to inform the design of competitive pay structures. In this sense, market pricing may be associated with conventional job evaluation in order to develop a pay system that is internally equitable as well as externally competitive. This is a desirable aim but one that may be difficult to achieve. Paying the competitive rate for a job can easily upset internal relativities as established by job evaluation.

But market pricing has a second meaning. It can denote a method of directly pricing jobs on the basis of external relativities with no regard to internal relativities. This was called 'extreme market pricing' by Ellis et al (2004). As a means of valuing jobs this can be regarded as a form of job evaluation, as it is in the United States. However, a strict definition of job evaluation – the one adopted in this book – is that a job evaluation scheme is solely concerned with internal relativities. Market pricing in its first sense as defined above is used separately to determine external relativities.

The rationale for extreme market pricing can be expressed in the adage 'a job is worth what the market says it is worth'. The only thing that counts is to be competitive and this governs the rates for individual jobs and the design of pay structures. Relativities within the organization reflect relativities in the marketplace. Extreme market pricing means that the organization does not need to bother with traditional job evaluation. As Zingheim and Schuster (2002) asserted: 'The history of pay involves entitlement disguised as a nearly singular emphasis on internal equity.' The future as they see it 'depends on our ability to develop and implement a base salary system that is anchored in the marketplace'. One of the problems of extreme market pricing is that relying on information about job relativities in the marketplace to determine internal relativities can lead to transmitting inequities from the marketplace to the organization, for example, between jobs filled mainly by women and those carried out mainly by men. Organizations that adopt an extreme market pricing approach can be described as 'market driven' and 16 per cent of the respondents to the 2017 e-reward job evaluation survey stated that they were in this category. Extreme market pricing is more prevalent in the United States than in the UK partly because equal pay legislation is weaker in the United States and partly for the reason given by Zingheim and Schuster – a fundamental belief in the supremacy of the market.

However, concerns about the legitimacy of extreme market pricing do not obviate the need for market rate analysis.

Requirements for effective market rate analysis

Market pricing depends on good market data, the validity and reliability of which is affected by three factors:

1 *Sample frame* – the degree to which the sample of organizations from which the data has been collected is fully representative of the organizations with which comparisons need to be made in such terms as sector, technology or type of business, size and location.

2 *Timing* – the extent to which the information is up to date or can be updated reliably. By their very nature, published surveys, upon which many people rely, can soon become out of date. This can happen the moment they are produced – pay levels may have changed and people may have moved in or out since the date of the survey. Whilst it is not possible to overcome this completely, as data must be gathered and analyzed, surveys which aim to have as short a time as possible between data collection and the publication of results are likely to be of more use than those with longer

lead times. Estimates can be made of likely movements since the survey took place, but they are mainly guesswork.

3 *Job matching* – the extent to which good job matching between internal and external jobs has taken place. Inadequate job matching is a major cause of inaccuracies in the data collected by market analysis. So far as possible the aim is to match the jobs within the organization and those outside (the comparators) so that like is being compared with like. It is essential to avoid crude and misleading comparisons based on job titles alone or vague descriptions of job content such as those contained in advertisements. It is first necessary to ensure that the sample frame is adequate – a broad match is needed between the organization and the types of organizations used as comparators in terms of sector, industry classification, size and location.

The various methods of job matching in ascending order of accuracy are:

- *Job title*: this can be misleading. Job titles by themselves give no indication of the range of duties or the level of responsibility and are sometimes used to convey additional status to employees or their customers unrelated to the real level of work done.

- *Brief description of duties and level or zone of responsibility*: national surveys frequently restrict their job-matching definitions to a two- or three-line description of duties and an indication of levels of responsibility in rank order. The latter is often limited to a one-line definition for each level or zone in a hierarchy. This approach provides some guidance on job matching, which reduces major discrepancies, but it still leaves considerable scope for discretion and can therefore provide only generalized comparisons.

- *Capsule job descriptions*: special surveys by groups of employers (pay clubs) and 'bespoke' surveys frequently use capsule job descriptions that define main responsibilities and duties in about 100 to 200 words. To increase the refinement of comparisons, modifying statements may be made indicating where responsibilities are higher or lower than the norm. Capsule job descriptions considerably increase the accuracy of comparisons as long as they are based on a careful analysis of actual jobs and include modifying statements. But they are not always capable of dealing with specialist jobs and the accuracy of comparisons in relation to levels of responsibility may be limited, even when modifiers are used.

- *Full job profiles*, including a factor analysis of the levels of responsibility involved, may be used in special surveys when direct comparisons are made between jobs in different organizations. They can be more accurate on a one-for-one basis but their use is limited because of the time and labour involved in preparing them. A further limitation is that comparator organizations may not have available, or be prepared to make available, their own for comparison.

- *Job evaluation* can be used in support of a capsule job description or a role profile to provide a more accurate measure of relative job size. A common method of evaluation is necessary and this is often provided through a management consultant's scheme. A number of international and UK consultancies now claim to be able to make this link, either through a point-factor scheme or a levelling approach. This approach will further increase the accuracy of comparisons but the degree of accuracy will depend on the quality of the job evaluation process.

The process of market analysis

The process of market analysis consists of the following steps:

1 Decide on the benchmark jobs for which market rate data will be collected.
2 Identify potential sources of market rate data and select the most appropriate ones.
3 Assemble the data.
4 Analyse and interpret the data from the various sources.

Decide on benchmark jobs

The survey should aim to collect data on a representative sample of benchmark jobs. The jobs selected should be ones for which it is likely that market data will be available. However, there are usually some jobs that are unique to the organization and for which comparisons cannot be made. When conducting a market pricing exercise it is necessary to make a judgement on the positioning of these jobs in the pay structure on the basis of comparisons with the benchmark jobs. A point-factor or matching evaluation scheme, if available, helps to make these comparisons more accurate.

Sources of market rate data

There is a wide variety of sources of varying quality and it is advisable to select more than one to ensure that a spread of information is obtained. Because it is unlikely that precise job matching, a perfect sample, and coincidence of timing will be achieved it is best to obtain data from more than one source. The 2013 WorldatWork survey found that over 40 per cent of respondents used three or more sources.

Ultimately, a judgement has to be made about market levels of pay and this will be helped if a range of information is available that enables a view to be taken on what should be regarded as 'the market rate' for internal use. This is more convincing if it has been derived from a number of sources and when this occurs it is called a 'derived market rate'. In choosing data sources it is important to take account of how easily replicable the analysis will be in future years. Trends can only be identified if a consistent set of sources is used and those sources are reasonably stable. A list of the main sources and their advantages and disadvantages is given in Table 10.1.

Published surveys that are readily accessible and are based on a large sample can be used to back up individual or club surveys. If the information can be obtained online, so much the better. But it has to be relevant to the needs of the organization and particular attention should always be paid to the range of data and the quality of job matching. General market data can be supplemented by specialist surveys covering particular jobs. Should the quality of job matching be important, an individual survey can be conducted or a pay club can be joined if there is room.

Market intelligence and published data from journals and associated sources should always be used as back-up material and for

Table 10.1   Analysis of data sources

Source	Brief description	Advantages	Disadvantages
Online data	Access data from general surveys.	Quick, easy, can be tailored.	May not provide all the information required.
General national published surveys	Available for purchase – provide an overall picture of pay levels for different occupations in national and regional labour markets.	Wide coverage, readily available, continuity allows trend analyses over time, expert providers.	Risk of imprecise job matching, insufficiently specific, quickly out of date.
Local published surveys	Available for purchase – provide an overall picture of pay levels for different occupations in the local labour market.	Focus on local labour market especially for administrative staff and manual workers.	Risk of imprecise job matching, insufficiently specific, quickly out of date, providers may not have expertise in pay surveys.
Sector surveys	Available for purchase – provide data on a sector such as charities.	Focus on a sector where pay levels may differ from national rates, deal with particular categories in depth.	Risk of imprecise job matching, insufficiently specific, quickly out of date.
Industrial/ occupational surveys	Surveys, often conducted by employer and trade associations on jobs in an industry or specific jobs.	Focus on an industry, deal with particular categories in depth, quality of job matching may be better than general or sector surveys.	Job matching may still not be entirely precise, quickly out of date.

(continued)

Table 10.1 *(Continued)*

Source	Brief description	Advantages	Disadvantages
Management consultants' databases	Pay data obtained from the databases maintained by management consultants.	Based on well-researched and matched data. Often highly tailored to specific market segments.	Only obtainable from specific consultants and often confidential to participants. Can be expensive.
Special surveys	Surveys specially conducted by an organization.	Focused, reasonably good job matching, control of participants, control of analysis methodology.	Takes time and trouble, may be difficult to get participation, sample size may therefore be inadequate. May not be repeated, therefore difficult to use for ongoing pay management
Pay clubs	Groups of employers who regularly exchange data on pay levels.	Focused, precise job matching, control of participants, control of analysis methodology, regular data, trends data, more information may be available on benefits and pay policies.	Sample size may be too small, involve a considerable amount of administration, may be difficult to maintain enthusiasm of participants.
Published data in journals	Data on settlements and pay levels available from IDS or XpertHR and on national trends in earnings from the New Earnings Survey.	Readily accessible.	Mainly about settlements and trends, little specific well-matched information on pay levels for individual jobs.

(continued)

Table 10.1 *(Continued)*

Source	Brief description	Advantages	Disadvantages
Analysis of recruitment data	Pay data derived from analysis of pay levels required to recruit staff.	Immediate data.	Data random and can be misleading because of small sample. Can be distorted if applicants inflate their salary history or if data geared to recruitment salaries.
Job advertisements	Pay data obtained from job advertisements.	Readily accessible, highly visible (to employees as well as employers), up to date. Data can be quite specific for public- and voluntary-sector roles.	Job matching very imprecise, pay information may be misleading.
Other market intelligence	Pay data obtained from informal contacts or networks.	Provide good background.	Imprecise, not regularly available.

information on going rates and trends. They can provide invaluable help with updating.

Although the analysis of job advertisements has its dangers, it can be used as further back-up, or to give an instant snapshot of current rates, but it is risky to rely on this source alone.

Published surveys are of widely varying content, presentation and quality and are sometimes expensive. When selecting a published survey use the following guidelines:

- Does it cover relevant jobs in similar organizations?

- Does it provide the information on the pay and benefits required?

- Are there enough participants to provide acceptable comparisons?

- So far as can be judged, is the survey conducted properly in terms of its sampling techniques and the quality of job matching?
- Is the survey reasonably up to date?
- Are the results well presented?
- Does it provide value for money?

Assemble data

A market rate analysis exercise needs to be project-managed, especially when data from a number of different sources has to be collected. Account should be taken of the publication dates of surveys and the time needed to conduct a special survey or generate information from a pay club.

Interpret and present market data

Data needs to be interpreted by reference to the details provided from each source and by assessments of its reliability, accuracy and relevance. If data has been obtained from a number of sources these will also have to be interpreted to produce a derived market rate, which will be used as the basis of comparison.

Limitations of market pricing

The effectiveness of market pricing depends on getting the right data – accurate information on the rates for jobs in the marketplace that can be matched with comparable jobs within the organization. The problem with achieving this ideal state is the nebulous nature of the concept of a market rate.

Establishing what the market rate for a job is can be a matter of judgement rather than certainty. All too many managers and senior executives – and, indeed, many employees – commonly believe that it is not only possible, but relatively easy, to establish a 'correct' rate for any given job, in any industry, in any location, for any age or experience level, preferably to the nearest pound. But accurate market rate information may be difficult to obtain. Pay data is based on complex decisions. It is rare for two companies, even within the same industry and location, to be managed in the same way. Different corporate values, variations in the 'pay stance' adopted by organizations (where they want their pay levels to be in relation to market rates), perceptions of the contribution of each job to the effectiveness of the organization, and the experience and performance of the individuals holding the jobs all impact on the remuneration paid to people in apparently similar positions.

Ultimately those differences are reflected in the market. There is always a choice of rates. No survey is able, despite the claims of some surveyors, to provide a single 'right' rate of pay for any position, or range of positions. Employees in effect have their own market rate, depending on their expertise and ability and the degree to which their talents are unique. This individual 'market worth' varies widely and is often as much a matter of perception as of fact. When making comparisons between internal and external rates for jobs the aim is to compare like with like. But it may be difficult or even impossible to obtain precise matches between jobs in the organization and jobs elsewhere. 'Like' jobs may not exist. The comparisons may be approximate and the outcome is that the range between the highest and lowest levels of pay for a job as established by an individual survey can be as much as 50 per cent or more. Different surveys will produce different results depending on the sample of organizations covered, the quality of matching and the timing of the survey.

The translation of pay market data into an acceptable company pay structure or competitive pay levels for individuals is a process based on intuition, judgement and compromise. Advocates of extreme market pricing believe that the only required feature of a pay policy is that it should be competitive. Internal equity is unimportant. They assert that it obviates the need for spurious attempts to establish comparative worth through formal job evaluation. They claim that market rates are ascertainable facts not subject to the judgements made using job evaluation schemes. However, this claim is specious; judgements have to be made about market rate data just as they have to be made in any type of job evaluation. Market pricing cannot guarantee valid results.

Market pricing means striking a balance between the competing merits of the different sources of data and extracting a 'derived market rate'. But the judgements will be more accurate if they are based on the systematic analysis of valid and reliable data gained from reputable published surveys, established 'pay clubs' or well-conceived surveys conducted by the organization.

Many people believe that a further limitation to market pricing is that it ignores principles of internal equity. They claim that a pay structure based on market pricing will distort internal relativities and lead to unequal pay. The counter-argument is that pay structures cannot ignore external relativities and the use of such devices as market supplements (payments in addition to the rate for a job as determined by internal equity which reflect market rates) will unavoidably create internal inequities. But when market supplements are used, at least the basic structure has been designed in accordance with the principle of establishing comparable worth and supplements can be identified as such and objectively justified. Moreover, it is generally recognized that reliance on market pricing is likely to reproduce within the organization existing inequities between the pay of men and women in the marketplace.

The facile assumptions of many of those who support extreme market pricing have been challenged by a number of commentators. Babcock et al (1996) highlighted the dangers with pay surveys of inaccurate matching of jobs and that the choice of pay comparators can carry the risk of 'self-serving bias', especially in formal negotiations over pay and conditions. Schmidt and Dworschak (2006) coined the term 'mimetic wages' to caricature the way many private-sector firms will seek only to mimic or match the wages of competitors without systematic analysis and primarily as a defensive retention strategy. Findlay et al (2013) noted that the choice of comparator significantly affects the outcome. And as Brown et al (2016) pointed out:

> For those saying they have abandoned inflexible job evaluation methods in favour of external market pay determination, the whole question of how surveys compare and measure jobs in order to gather their pay level data, other than simple alignment of job titles, makes this a somewhat tautological argument.

Such attacks on the naïve assumption that extreme market pricing is an easy solution to the problem of maintaining a competitive pay structure may be justified. But it is still necessary to track market rates in order to take account of them when making decisions on pay levels and structures. What must be recognized is that it is essential to make every effort to achieve a good match when making comparisons and to set up an appropriate sample frame. It is also necessary to remember that market rate information will seldom if ever be definitive and that judgement and approximation are required when assessing the results of market rate surveys.

References

Babcock, L, Xianghong, W and Lowenstein, G (1996) Choosing the wrong pond: social comparisons in negotiations that reflect a self-serving bias, *The Quarterly Journal of Economics*, **111** (1), pp 1–19

Brown D, Bevan, S and Rickard, C (2016) A review of pay comparability methodologies, Institute for Employment Studies [Online] https://www.gov.uk/government/publications/a-review-of-pay-comparability-methodologies [accessed 1 May 2017]

CIPD (2017) Market pricing and job evaluation [Online] https://www.cipd.co.uk/knowledge/strategy/reward/market-pricing-factsheet [accessed 26 May 2017]

Ellis, C M, Laymon, R G and LeBlanc, P V (2004) Improving pay productivity with strategic work valuation, *WorldatWork Journal*, Second Quarter, pp 56–68

e-reward (2017) *Survey of Job Evaluation*, Stockport, e-reward

Findlay, J, Findlay, P and Stewart, R (2014) Occupational pay comparisons – easier said than done? *Employee Relations*, **36** (1), pp 2–16

Schmidt, W and Dworschak, B (2006) Pay developments in Britain and Germany: collective bargaining, 'benchmarking' and 'mimetic' wages', *European Journal of Industrial Relations*, **12** (1), pp 89–109

WorldatWork (2013) *Job Evaluation and Market Pricing Practices*, Scottsdale, AZ, WorldatWork

XpertHR (2012), *Using Market-pay Comparisons*, London, XpertHR

Zingheim, P K and Schuster, J R (2002) Pay changes going forward, *Compensation & Benefits Review*, **34** (4), pp 48–53

PART THREE
Applications of job evaluation

Developing grade and pay structures

11

The outcome of a job evaluation exercise is usually a new or revised grade and pay structure. The purpose of this chapter is to describe how job evaluation contributes to the design process for the various types of structures. The chapter starts with definitions of grade and pay structures. It then describes how job evaluation is used in their design – generally and for particular structures. Equal value considerations are dealt with at the end of the chapter.

Grade and pay structures

Grade and pay structures provide a framework within which an organization's pay policies can be implemented. They enable the organization to determine where jobs should be placed in a hierarchy, define pay levels and the scope for pay progression and provide the basis upon which relativities can be managed, equal pay achieved and the processes of monitoring and controlling the implementation of pay practices can take place. A grade and pay structure can also serve as a medium through which the organization communicates the career and pay opportunities available to employees.

Grade structures

A grade structure consists of a sequence or hierarchy of grades, bands or levels into which groups of jobs which are broadly comparable in value or size are placed. There may be a single structure, which is defined by the number of grades or bands it contains. Alternatively, the structure may be divided into a number of families consisting of groups of jobs where the essential nature and purpose of the work are similar but the work is carried out at different levels.

The main types of graded structures are:

- *Multi-graded structures* – which consist of a sequence of narrow grades (generally 10 or more). They are also known as narrow-graded structures.

- *Broad-graded structures* – which have fewer grades (generally six to nine).

- *Broad-banded structures* – which consist of a limited number of bands (often four to five). Structures with six or more grades are often described as broad-banded even when their characteristics are typical of broad grades.

- *Job family structures* – which consist of a number of groups of jobs with similar characteristics, each divided typically into six to eight levels. The levels are described in terms of key responsibilities and knowledge, skill, and competence requirements, and therefore define career progression routes within and between families. There may be a common grade and pay structure across all the families, or pay levels in each family may differ to reflect market rate considerations (this is sometimes referred to as market grouping). The number of levels in families may also vary.

- *Pay spines* consisting of a series of incremental 'pay points' extending from the lowest- to the highest-paid jobs covered by the structure.

Many organizations do not have a graded structure at all for any jobs or for certain jobs such as directors. Instead they use 'spot rates' or 'individual job ranges'. A spot rate is the pay for a job or an individual which is not fitted into a grade or band in a conventional grade structure and does not allow any scope for pay progression. An individual job range is a spot rate in which there is a defined range for pay progression.

Grades, bands or levels may be defined in one or other of the following ways or a combination of them:

- by means of a range of job evaluation points – jobs are allocated to a grade, band or level if their job evaluation scores fall within a range or bracket of points;

- in words which describe the characteristics of the work carried out in the jobs that are positioned in each grade or level – these grade, band or level definitions, often called 'profiles', may set out the key activities and the competences or knowledge and skills required at different points in the hierarchy;

- by reference to benchmark jobs or roles that have already been placed in the grade, band or job family level.

Designing grade structures

The design of a grade structure involves deciding on the number of levels required and then defining each level to provide guidance on the level appropriate for the job being evaluated. As discussed below, the approaches used differ according to what type of scheme is used, either matching/levelling or point-factor. These methods are also used in the design of a job family structure as described in the next section of this chapter.

Grade structure design when a job-to-grade matching or a levelling approach is used

In job-to-grade matching, the structure design can be based on an *a priori* view that is made empirically by reference to the existing hierarchy or a belief that the present number of grades should be reduced to a more manageable number. It is preferable to base the decision on a ranking of benchmark posts, possibly using paired comparisons, and an analysis of the clustering of jobs based on the identification of common characteristics. The ranked jobs are then divided into grades according to views on the number of distinct levels of responsibility that exist in the organization. The descriptors for each level of the structure (the level or grade profiles) generally refer to the factors or elements used in the scheme (an example is given in Chapter 8, Table 8.3).

In the DMA version of levelling as described in Chapter 9 the structure is pre-determined by reference to the hierarchy of distinct levels of accountability in the organization.

Grade structure design following a point-factor job evaluation exercise

A structure can be designed following a point-factor job evaluation exercise that will produce a rank order of jobs according to their scores. A decision then has to be made on where the boundaries that will define grades should be placed in the rank order. So far as possible, boundaries should divide groups or clusters of jobs which are significantly different in size so that all the jobs placed in a grade are clearly larger than the jobs placed in the next lower grade and smaller than the jobs in the next higher grade. But this process is not scientific and it is rare to find a situation where there is one right and obvious answer.

A method that is often recommended is to analyse the distribution of scores in an attempt to identify any significant gaps in the scores between adjacent jobs. These natural breaks, if there are any, will then constitute the boundaries between clusters of jobs that can be allocated to adjacent grades. A distinct gap between the highest-rated job in one grade and the lowest-rated job in the grade above will help to justify the allocation of jobs between grades. It will therefore reduce boundary problems leading to dissatisfaction with gradings when the distinction is less well defined. However, in practice, convenient clusters of jobs that form natural breaks may not exist.

In these circumstances the following guidelines should be considered when deciding on boundaries:

- Jobs with common features as indicated by the job evaluation factors are grouped together so that a distinction can be made between the characteristics of the jobs in different grades – it should be possible to demonstrate that the jobs grouped into one grade resemble each other more than they resemble jobs placed in adjacent grades.

- The grade hierarchy should take account of the organizational hierarchy, ie jobs in which the job holder reports to a higher-level job holder should normally be placed in a lower grade although this principle cannot be followed slavishly when an organization is over-hierarchical with, perhaps, a series of one-over-one reporting relationships.

- Ideally the boundaries should not be positioned immediately above jobs in which large numbers of people are employed, or if they are, there needs to be a convincing reason for the positioning of the boundary otherwise it may be difficult to resist the large number of requests for upgrading that may take place.

- The boundaries should not be placed between jobs mainly carried out by men and jobs mainly carried out by women.

- The grade width in terms of job evaluation points should represent a significant step in demand as indicated by the job evaluation scheme – there is no need for each grade to have the same number of points, but if there are large differences between grades the reasons for creating such differences may be subject to question.

By far the majority of the respondents to the 2017 e-reward job evaluation survey (68 per cent) allocate jobs to grades or bands by reference to definitions of grade boundaries expressed in terms of job evaluation points. The rest use some form of matching.

An example of a structure based on a point-factor scheme is given in Chapter 8, Table 8.4.

The role of job evaluation in the design of job family structures

The design of a job family structure starts by a decision on what separate families should be included in the structure. These may consist of the major functions but when there are some linked occupations that are particularly subject to market rate pressures, they can be treated as separate market groups so that competitive rates of pay can be fixed for the jobs concerned. The grades within job families are defined in the same way as those in a conventional structure, ie either by a range of job evaluation scores or by a grade profile. But profiles will focus on knowledge, skill and ability (KSA) requirements at each level in order to define career paths.

Pay structures

Pay structures define the different levels of pay for jobs or groups of jobs by reference to their relative internal value as determined by job evaluation, to external relativities as established by market rate surveys and, sometimes, to negotiated rates for jobs. They provide scope for pay progression in accordance with performance, competence, contribution or service.

A grade structure becomes a pay structure when pay ranges, brackets or scales are attached to each grade, band or level. In some broad-graded structures, 'grades within grades' or pay zones are established to limit the scope for pay progression and to align pay to the market rates for the job or jobs placed in the sub-grade.

Pay structures are defined by the number of grades they contain and, especially in narrow-graded structures, the span or width of the pay ranges attached to each grade. Span is the scope the grade provides for pay progression and is usually measured as the difference between the lowest point and highest point in the range as a percentage of the lowest point. Thus a range of £30,000 to £39,000 would have a span of 30 per cent. Elliott Jaques (1961) suggested that this was the optimum range.

Developing pay structures

Multi-graded structures may have pay ranges of, typically, 25 per cent to 40 per cent attached to each grade or level. All jobs placed in a particular grade will be paid within the range for that grade and will progress through the range on the basis of performance, competence, contribution or service. Progression within a range may be limited by thresholds that can only be crossed if defined levels of performance and competence have been achieved. The pay ranges are determined by reference to the existing rates of pay for the jobs allocated to each grade and their market rates. An analysis of market rates forms part of the pay structure design programme but in practice it may not always be possible to get reliable information for all the jobs, especially those for which good external matches are difficult to make.

Designing a multi-graded pay structure

The following steps are required to design a multi-graded pay structure:

1 List the jobs placed within each grade on the basis of job evaluation (these might be limited to benchmark jobs that have been evaluated but there must be an adequate number of them if a proper basis for the design is to be provided).

2 Establish the actual rates of pay of the job holders.

3 For each grade, set out the range of pay for job holders and calculate their average or median rate of pay (the pay practice point). It is helpful to plot this pay practice data as illustrated in Figure 11.1, which shows pay in each grade against job evaluation scores and includes a pay practice trend line.

4 Obtain information on the market rates for benchmark jobs where available. If possible this should indicate the median rate and the upper and lower quartiles.

5 Agree policy on how the organization's pay levels should relate to market rates – its 'market stance'. This could be at the median, or above the median if it is believed that pay levels should be more competitive.

6 Calculate the average market rates for the benchmark jobs in each grade according to pay stance policy, eg the median rates. This produces the range market reference point.

7 Compare the practice and market reference points in each range and decide on the range reference point. This usually becomes the midpoint of the pay range for the grade and is regarded as the target or competitive rate for a fully competent job holder in that grade. This is a judgemental process, which takes into account the difference

Figure 11.1   Scattergram of evaluations and pay

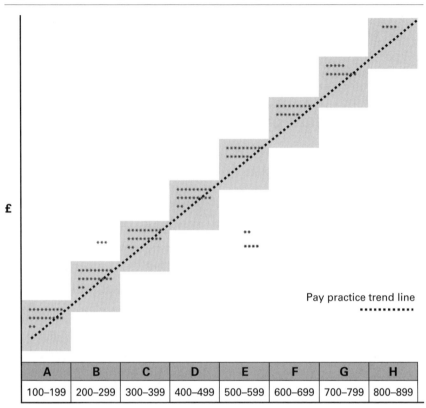

A	B	C	D	E	F	G	H
100–199	200–299	300–399	400–499	500–599	600–699	700–799	800–899

between the practice and policy points, the perceived need to be more competitive if policy rates are higher, and the likely costs of increasing rates.

8 Examine the pay differentials between reference points in adjacent grades. These should provide scope to recognize increases in job size and, so far as possible, variations between differentials should be kept to a minimum. If differentials are too close – less than 10 per cent – many jobs become borderline cases, which can result in a proliferation of appeals and arguments about grading. Large differentials below senior management level of more than 25 per cent can create problems for marginal or borderline cases because of the amount at stake. Experience has shown that in most organizations with conventional grade structures a differential of between 15 and 20 per cent is appropriate except, perhaps, at the highest levels.

9 Decide on the range of pay around the reference point. A conventional arrangement is to allow 15 per cent on either side, thus if the reference point is 100 per cent, the range is from 85 per cent to 115 per cent (a span of 35 per cent). The range can, however, vary in accordance with policy on the scope for progression and if a given range of pay has to be covered by the structure, the fewer the grades the wider the ranges.

10 Decide on the extent, if any, to which pay ranges should overlap. Overlap recognizes that an experienced job holder at the top of a range may be making a greater contribution than an inexperienced job holder at the lower end of the range above. Large overlaps of more than 10 per cent can create equal pay problems where, for example, men are clustered at the top of their grades and women are more likely to be found at the lower end.

11 Review the impact of the above pay range decisions on the pay of existing staff. Formulate protection and assimilation policies. Protection policies usually guarantee that no one loses any pay after a new structure is introduced. Assimilation policies cover how individuals will be fitted into a revised pay structure (further details on these policies were given in Chapter 5). Establish the number of staff whose present rate of pay is above or below the pay range for the grade into which their jobs have been placed and the extent of the difference between the rate of pay of those below the minimum and the lowest point of that pay range. Calculate the costs of bringing them up to the minimum. Bearing in mind protection and assimilation policies, the introduction of a new structure almost inevitably results in an increase in payroll costs – the pay of some people will go up but no one's pay will go down. Typically, these costs amount to about 3 per cent of payroll. They can be managed down but with difficulty.

12 When the above steps have been completed it may be necessary to review the decisions made on the grade structure and pay reference points and ranges. Iteration is almost always necessary to obtain a satisfactory result from the viewpoint of its cost and how it affects individuals.

Deciding on pay ranges and levels in broad-graded or banded structures

Where the number of grades or bands is limited, which may well be the case if a levelling exercise as described in Chapter 9 has taken place, it will be difficult if not impossible to have pay spans extending over the whole range. In these circumstances, as noted by Brown et al (2016):

> Market surveys generally play a key role in determining what range of pay staff in particular functions and locations are paid. In many cases local 'grades within levels' are developed to practically manage pay within such broad bands – with literally dozens of ranges for different roles within some of Tesco's levels for example.

A grade within a level generally takes the form of an individual job range where the mid-point is aligned to the market rate for the job – market pricing – and the range extends on either side, typically by 15 per cent of the mid-point.

Deciding on pay ranges and levels in job family structures

A job family structure can consist of separate job families, each of which has its own grade and pay structure that takes account of different levels of market rates between families (sometimes called 'market grouping'); or they can consist of different career paths and pay ranges overlaid onto a common grading structure. The size of jobs and rates of pay can vary between the same levels in different job families. Job family structures help organizations to flex pay rates for different occupations to reflect variations in market rates as well as helping to define career paths within job families. Pay levels in job families are usually determined by market pricing.

References

Brown, D, Bevan, S and Rickard, C (2016) A review of pay comparability methodologies, Institute for Employment Studies [Online] https://www.gov. uk/government/publications/a-review-of-pay-comparability-methodologies [accessed 1 May 2017]

e-reward (2017) *Job Evaluation Survey*, Stockport, e-reward

Jaques, E (1961) *Equitable Payment*, London, Heinemann

Equal pay 12

Job evaluation has particular significance when it refers to the achievement of equal pay for work of equal value between women and men – the main focus of this chapter. But the approaches to achieving equal pay covered by the chapter are just as applicable to other forms of potential pay discrimination including between people of different races, religions, ages and sexual orientations, and those with disabilities and those without.

The gap between the pay of men and women is created by a number of factors in addition to direct discrimination between the base pay rates of men and women for like jobs. The causes of inequality also include other aspects of sex discrimination such as the fact that women tend to be clustered towards the bottom of organizational hierarchies and pay ranges while men tend to be clustered towards the top. The UK Equal Pay Task Force (2001) expressed the view that pay discrimination only contributed to 25 to 50 per cent of the pay gap. To reduce the pay gap it is therefore necessary to address issues concerning equal opportunity, pay progression systems, fixing rates of pay on appointment or promotion, and deciding on rates of pay when returning to work after pregnancy. But it is still important to prevent direct pay discrimination. Job evaluation has a major part to play in this by establishing when jobs are equal in value and should therefore be paid equally and by underpinning equal pay reviews designed to analyse the size of pay gaps and assist in the diagnosis of their causes.

The role of job evaluation in achieving equal pay in the UK is carried out within the framework of equal pay law as summarized in the first part of this chapter. The next four parts deal respectively with how to avoid discrimination in job evaluation, defending an equal pay claim in the UK, managing the risk of an equal pay claim, and conducting an equal pay review.

Equal pay law in the UK

The Equal Pay Act (1970) ended the previously common practice of employers paying men and women different amounts of money for doing jobs that were either the same or very similar. It became unlawful to operate separate male and female pay scales or to pay men and women differently for doing jobs that should have been paid at the same grade when a job evaluation system was in operation. Later, in 1983 after the UK joined the European Union, it became possible for employees to pursue claims in an employment tribunal when they believed that their work, despite being different in nature from that of a comparator of the opposite sex, was nonetheless of 'equal value to his or hers'. The relevant law is now all found in the Equality Act 2010. It applies both to men and to women, but in practice the large majority of cases are brought by or on behalf of women.

Aside from these three headings under which a claim can be brought (ie like work, work that has been rated as equivalent, and work of equal value), the Equality Act sets out the major defences that are available to employers. The most widely deployed is known as the 'material factor defence' which involves satisfying the tribunal that the difference in the level of payment between the claimant and her comparator is genuinely explained by factors that have nothing to do with gender.

Partly, if not largely, as a result of this law the 'gender pay gap' between male and female workers in the UK has declined from 37 per cent in the early 1970s to around 18 per cent today, depending on how it is measured. The reasons for its persistence despite the presence of equal pay law are widely debated, a number of distinct and plausible explanations having been put forward. One possibility is the requirement that the law places on women to challenge their employers either by threatening or actually taking legal action. This is a difficult path for any employee to take and one that, quite understandably, most are reluctant to embark on. Moreover, in many workplaces quite strict confidentiality rules have the effect of deterring people from telling their colleagues about the true level of their earnings. As a result, even if someone was willing to challenge unequal payments between men and women, their ability to do so effectively has been seriously curtailed.

Important reforms aimed at reducing this barrier and putting pressure on employers to act proactively in respect of equalizing pay are going to be phased in over a number of years after 2016. These will eventually require all organizations employing more than 250 people to undertake equal pay audits and to publish details of any gender pay gap among their workers on their websites. Not only will this make it much harder for employers to hide details of any gender pay gap that they operate, but it may in many cases simply serve to alert them when they are paying unlawfully in a manner which is legally difficult to justify. The new law is thus likely to have the effect of further reducing the pay gap between men and women.

Defending an equal pay claim in the UK

The two most common grounds for defending a claim in the UK are (1) that the work is not equal and (2) that even if it is equal, there is a genuine material factor that justifies the difference in pay. Employers cannot defend equal value cases on the grounds of the cost of implementation or the effect a decision could have on industrial relations, and part-time working per se cannot provide a defence to a claim. An employment tribunal can ask an independent expert to analyse the jobs and report on whether or not they are of equal value.

Proving that the work is not equal through the job evaluation study defence

The onus is on the employer to prove that the complainant is not carrying out like work, work rated as equivalent or work of equal value when compared with the comparator. If the employer invokes job evaluation to provide support to a claim that the jobs are not equal (the job evaluation study defence), the scheme must be analytical, unbiased and applied in a non-discriminatory way. The 'job evaluation study defence' applies only where applicant and comparator jobs are covered by the same job evaluation scheme.

Analytical means that the scheme must analyse and compare jobs by reference to factors such as, in the words of the UK Equal

Pay Regulations, 'effort, skill, decision'. Slotting jobs on a whole-job comparison basis is not acceptable as a defence. The legislation and case law does not specify that a point-factor or a scored factor comparison scheme should be used but even if an 'analytical matching' process is followed a tribunal may need to be convinced that this is analytical within the meaning of the Act and has not led to biased decisions.

The genuine material factor defence

UK law provides for a case to be made by the employer that there is a 'genuine material factor' creating the difference between the pay of the applicant and the comparator that can be objectively justified. A genuine material factor could be the level of performance or length of service of the comparator, which means that he or she is paid at a higher level than the applicant in the pay range for a job, or it could be the need to respond to market rate pressures. But this only applies if the basis for deciding on additions to pay and the process of doing so are not discriminatory.

Pay differences arising from market pricing can possibly be treated as genuine material factors as long as they are 'objectively justified'. In the case of a claim that market pressures justify unequal pay the tribunal will need to be convinced that this was not simply a matter of opinion and that adequate evidence from a number of sources was available. In such cases, the tribunal will also require proof that the recruitment and retention of the people required by the organization was difficult because pay levels were uncompetitive.

Managing the risk of equal pay claims

Some organizations in low-risk situations may be convinced that they are doing enough about ensuring equal pay without introducing job evaluation. Others have decided that because their business imperatives are pressing they are prepared to accept a measure of risk in their policy on equal pay, especially when they are aware that in the private sector at least, equal pay claims are much less frequent.

Some, regrettably, may not care. But if there is some risk then action needs to be taken to minimize it. Successful equal pay claims can be hugely expensive, especially in UK public-sector organizations with powerful and active trade unions. Equal pay risk management may therefore involve using a non-discriminatory job evaluation scheme and conducting equal pay reviews as described in the final section of this chapter. Equal pay risk assessment involves considering two factors: (1) the risk of having to defend an equal pay claim and (2) the risk of a claim being successful.

Assessing the risk of a claim means first analysing the extent to which there is unequal pay and if it does exist, diagnosing the cause(s). These could be any of the following:

- different base rates of pay for work of equal value;
- disproportionate distribution of men or women at the upper or lower part of a pay range or an incremental scale, bearing in mind that this is a major cause of unequal pay;
- men or women placed at higher points on the scale on appointment or promotion;
- men or women receive higher merit or performance pay awards or benefit more from accelerated increments;
- market supplements applied differentially to men or women;
- 'red or green circling' applied in a way that results in pay discrimination between men and women doing work of equal value or like work;
- a discriminating job evaluation scheme in terms of factors or weightings or the job evaluation scheme is applied in a discriminatory way.

The best way to make this assessment is to carry out a formal equal pay review. If an organization is unwilling or unable to take this step, it should at least carry out an analysis of the pay of men and women carrying out like work to identify the existence and cause of any unjustified differences.

Secondly, assessing the risk of a claim means considering the possibility of an individual initiating action on their own or trade unions taking action on behalf of their members. Individual actions may come out of the blue but the individual may have raised an equal pay grievance formally or informally and line managers should understand that they must report this immediately to HR or senior management. A clear indication of trouble brewing in the UK is when an employee under the Employment Act 2002 submits an Equal Pay questionnaire to request information about whether their remuneration is equal to that of colleagues. Although trade unions are most likely to lodge questionnaires on behalf of their members, individuals can still do so independently by obtaining advice from the Equal Opportunities Commission (available on their website). The likelihood of trade union action will clearly be higher when there is a strong union with high penetration in the organization, which is often the case in the public sector. But any union member can seek help from her or his union. Even if the union is not recognized for negotiating purposes it can still provide support.

Equal pay reviews and job evaluation

Equal pay reviews establish whether any gender-related pay inequities have arisen, analyse the nature of any inequities, diagnose their cause or causes and determine what action is required to deal with them. In the UK they are mandatory in civil service departments and agencies.

Equal pay reviews take place in three stages:

1 *Analysis*: the collection and analysis of relevant data to identify any gender gaps.

2 *Diagnosis*: the process of reviewing gender gaps, understanding why they have occurred and what remedial action might be required if the differences cannot be objectively justified.

3 *Action*: agreeing and implementing an action plan that eliminates any inequalities.

Job evaluation can play a major part in the analysis stage. The analysis options are:

- *Like work* – this means identifying jobs anywhere in the organization where the work is the same or broadly similar. When there is no job evaluation this is the only type of equal work comparison that can readily be made. Although this should be a straightforward comparison there are potential pitfalls, such as over-reliance on unrepresentative job titles. If existing job titles are not a good guide, it might be necessary to re-categorize jobs in order to arrive at who is doing 'like work'.

- *Work rated as equivalent* – this means work that has been rated as equivalent using the organization's own analytical job evaluation scheme. Clearly analyses can only be readily applied where the organization has a job evaluation scheme that covers the whole organization.

- *Work of equal value* – this is the 'catch all' in equal pay legislation. It means that an equal pay claim can be brought by any employee where they believe that their job is of equal worth to any other role in the organization that is occupied by someone of the opposite sex. As with the 'work rated as equivalent' test the only organizations that can readily conduct analyses under this heading are those with an organization-wide job evaluation scheme that enables different types of jobs to be compared using criteria that apply equally across the organization.

Using job evaluation

If job evaluation is used on an organization-wide basis it is possible to conduct pay gap analyses that meet all three equal work categories. This can be done by conducting both a like work and an organization-wide comparison between the pay for men and women in the same grade irrespective of their occupational groups. This is because where organizations use analytical job evaluation, different types of jobs on the same grade defined in terms of a range of job evaluation scores will generally be regarded as being of 'equal worth', thus enabling a pay gap analysis that covers all employees in the same grade.

However, this is unlikely to be a satisfactory assessment of equal worth where bands or grades are so broad that they include jobs with a wide range of responsibilities and skills. Where this is the case, it may be necessary to split the grades/bands into narrower groups. This can be done fairly easily using a point-factor scheme's total job scores, but will not be so straightforward where other job evaluation techniques have been used (eg matching), without some adaptation to the scheme or alternative approach to deriving additional levels. Of course, the type of job evaluation approach used also impacts on the perceived robustness of the equal worth comparison in the first place.

Reference

Equal Pay Task Force (2001) *Just Pay: Report of the Equal Pay Task Force to the Equal Opportunities Commission*, Manchester, EOC

PART FOUR
The practice of job evaluation

Maintaining job 13
evaluation

The processes described in earlier chapters are necessary when consideration is being given to introducing job evaluation for the first time or substantially changing an existing arrangement. But job evaluation needs to be maintained on a continuing basis.

Organizations tend to heave a collective sigh of relief once the final job has been evaluated and graded and the last pay anomaly dealt with, assuming job evaluation can now be put to one side. It is not like that.

Some organizations fear that a job evaluation programme is like painting the Forth Bridge – as soon as you have got to the end you have to start again at the beginning. This inference of an inevitable, perpetual grind of evaluations is also wrong.

The Fort Bridge analogy is, however, relevant if looked at in the right way. The more thorough the preparation, the more care with which the materials are chosen and the more attention paid to their application, the longer it will take before any repainting is required. Regular inspections should identify those spots where things are getting flaky and prompt action should prevent the problem spreading. Some areas protected from the elements will last almost indefinitely while other areas will need continual touching up. The use of improved techniques will ensure better coverage and adapting the paint composition to meet changing conditions will mean that a total repaint will not be necessary for a long time. Maintaining job evaluation is very much like that.

Advice on maintaining job evaluation

The views of respondents to the 2017 e-reward survey on how to maintain job evaluation are set out below.

Do:

- allow appeals from employees if they think their job is under-graded;
- allow for some flexibility of process;
- audit/test regularly – review jobs annually;
- be as consistent as possible – any exceptions should be fully justified;
- be realistic about the resources required;
- ensure it is carried out by trained evaluators and carry out sore thumbing/moderation of JE scores over time to ensure consistency of application;
- refresh conventions;
- carry out periodic reviews and refresher communications and training;
- ensure you draw up notes for guidance as you do more role analysis, capturing the rationales for scoring;
- ensure good processes are in place;
- adhere to rules of the evaluation scheme and prevent ad hoc 'fudges' to the process for people fit rather than job size fit;
- ensure that gradings are robust and not unduly influenced, otherwise grade drift will happen and the scheme will lack credibility;
- make sure that once roles are evaluated, the evaluations are kept up to date with significant changes and new roles are evaluated prior to recruitment activity and offers being made;
- frequently review benchmark roles as still being fit for purpose as the business and roles employed develop;
- keep good accessible records of roles evaluated in each area and the reasons behind the scoring;
- ensure one person oversees the scheme and is a point of contact so all jobs evaluated are logged for future record keeping;
- ensure line managers and HR managers can 'self-serve' with more trained validation;

- ensure managers think about existing roles when evaluating and new and knock-on impacts;
- ensure people are trained properly for making judgements;
- make sure that there is a process for moderation;
- find benchmark jobs that can be tested externally.

Don't:

- allow the scheme to be abused;
- allow managers to influence the integrity of the scheme;
- allow job grades to be changed without due process;
- allow the methods to stray from the original training – be consistent;
- assume that one lot of training is enough for the operators – keep going;
- assume the scheme will last forever;
- be afraid to adapt the system – the core principles shouldn't change but the process can be simplified once staff are more comfortable with how it operates;
- be tempted to cut corners and slot jobs in – stick to the principles you've established;
- create a central black box where there is no understanding of how you got to the result;
- create pay ranges for each and every role based on market data, too onerous to refresh regularly to the market data – depending on how broad you want ranges to be you could have special ones for specific job families if necessary;
- let people with axes to grind have a say – be careful of role analysts who think they know what a job should be if it is at variance from what's written in the record;
- forget that your panel may need refresher training sessions – make sure you have budget to one side for this;
- forget to review the scheme to keep it relevant to the organization (review one family per year after one to two years);

- get dragged into piecemeal changes, as evaluation is about relativities – it's always important to look at roles in context and this is difficult with one-off reviews here and there;
- keep it as a Black Box secretive tool;
- let job evaluation, re-grading and committees become a cottage industry;
- have poor record keeping or lack of regular calibration consistency checking;
- over-complicate or duplicate work – one spreadsheet should be fine;
- let it sit there until you reach a real crisis with it;
- think that once you have something created it's going to work forever – be agile in thinking and updating;
- lose control – or provide too much autonomy;
- allow too many re-evaluations of the same job;
- ignore changes to jobs;
- forget to review the scheme to ensure it remains fit for purpose;
- let managers try to manipulate the system by pre-judging what grade the role should be;
- make exceptions which undermine the process;
- sacrifice the integrity of the process for expediency.

Reference

e-reward (2017) *Survey of Job Evaluation*, Stockport, e-reward

Issues and trends in job evaluation

14

Job evaluation is in a state of flux. The issues and trends that affect its use and future are assessed in this chapter.

Issues

The main issue in job evaluation today is 'Why should we use it at all?' In the United States the answer has on the whole been 'We don't need it'. Market pricing predominates. As the 2013 WorldatWork survey revealed, market pricing continues to well outpace all other methods as the dominant form of job evaluation with between 67 and 73 per cent prevalence, depending on job category.

It is different in the United Kingdom. XpertHR's 2013 job evaluation survey revealed that 71 per cent of UK organizations used a formal job evaluation scheme and 76 per cent of the respondents to the 2017 e-reward survey had one. And as Brown and Dive (2009) commented:

> By evolving to meet the needs of organizations for more fluid structures, more market- and person-driven pay and more talented leaders – as well as performing its traditional function as a foundation for fair pay management – job evaluation seems to be securing its place in the HR professional's toolkit for the foreseeable future.

However, The Institute for Employment Studies (Brown et al, 2016) noted: 'The persistence of job evaluation can largely be attributed not to the need to set internal pay levels and underpin pay surveys, but to the requirement to comply with equal pay law.' XpertHR's survey found that 69 per cent of organizations stated that the need to be equal pay compliant was behind their reason for using job evaluation. But the respondents to the 2017 e-reward job evaluation survey had different views. Their two top objectives for job evaluation were to help manage internal job relativities and to provide a basis for the design and maintenance of rational and defensible pay structure.

However, as the 2016 research by The Institute for Employment Studies found:

> In some sectors such as technology and parts of financial services there is very limited evidence of any job evaluation at all and in generally flatter organizations with more skills- and performance-based pay progression, pay determination is heavily external-market driven and market surveys play the key role in determining job worth.

In the UK there are two other issues. First, should a scheme be analytical or non-analytical? Second, what can be done about traditional methods of point-factor evaluation, which many believe to be over-complex and bureaucratic? The response to the first question is a preference for analytical schemes, because they are perceived to be more accurate but also, importantly, because they can provide a defence in an equal pay claim. The second question has been answered by a move away from point-factor rating as discussed below.

Trends

Job evaluation still exists, although Brown et al (2016) suggested that its role has declined in prominence, acting as a defensive barrier to equal pay claims rather than being a strong determinant of pay levels in detailed multi-graded structures. They noted:

> Contemporary developments have seen a shift towards more externally driven pay determination approaches informed by market pay surveys. These highlight a growing divergence across external markets in how and how much employers reward particular skill sets and occupations at an equivalent job size and level.

Large employers are devoting proportionately more resources to external market surveys and data and relatively less to job evaluation. They are taking more account of external data and 'vertical' divisions and variations in this for different functions and occupations and are less concerned with internal relativities. As Brown and Munday (2016) observed: 'Job evaluation operates in a supportive role, establishing a framework for pay management rather than controlling pay levels.'

The overall trend is for more pragmatic adaptation rather than revolution; for simplification rather than complexity. Analytical matching or levelling schemes are becoming popular – they were used by 68 per cent of the respondents to the 2017 e-reward survey. Point-factor schemes may be relegated to an underpinning role or abandoned completely. This development has been caused by the desire to simplify the process and to reduce the time-consuming nature of point-factor schemes applied to all jobs. Brown and Munday commented:

> Points factor evaluation may still be undertaken for difficult or contro-
> versial jobs, but most jobs are simply slotted into the appropriate level,
> and then the focus is on developing people's skills and contribution,
> which drives their pay progression up clearly communicated career
> pathways. Managers understand and accept banding decisions, while
> employees are engaged by the clarity and links between their pay
> progression and development of their skills and talents.

As Brown et al pointed out, pay consultants are also increasingly referring to job 'levelling' rather than job evaluation. Job levelling involves the definition of the levels in an organization using a stand-ard set of descriptors, often including competencies.

Changes to existing job evaluation systems were planned by 28 per cent of the respondents to the 2017 e-reward survey. Many of these were moving to levelling or job slotting. Proposed changes included:

- 'Considering other options for ranking and sizing roles rather than just points based.'
- 'In midst of switching from full Hay JE to using Hay job mapping.'
- 'Introducing job levels so roles are not specifically matched to individual job match codes.'

- 'Moving to a career framework and job evaluation will be done using levelling.'
- 'Looking to introduce job slotting.'
- 'Likely to move to work levels. Our current points methodology may still be used to underpin the new scheme, however.'
- 'We are changing our grading structures and will define anchor jobs at each new level, which we can then benchmark new jobs against to align them to the appropriate level.'
- 'Improve job matching to survey jobs of main vendors and correlation of internal levels to vendor levels.'

This move away from a total reliance on point-factor schemes to the use of matching or levelling is the most important development in recent years. Organizations such as the NHS and some universities often start with a point-factor scheme but rely mainly on job matching or slotting after the initial benchmark evaluations have taken place. Point-factor evaluation is only used when matching is difficult. Others may do without an underpinning point-factor job evaluation scheme altogether, relying on analytical matching or levelling.

References

Brown, D and Dive, B (2009) Level pegging, *People Management*, 15 January, pp 26–29

Brown, D and Munday, S (2016) *Stability rhymes with agility, pay structure needs to go with flexibility*, Opinion Paper 26, Institute for Employment Studies

Brown, D, Bevan, S and Rickard, C (2016) A review of pay comparability methodologies, Institute for Employment Studies [Online] https://www.gov.uk/government/publications/a-review-of-pay-comparability-methodologies [accessed 1 May 2017]

e-reward (2017) *Job Evaluation Survey*, Stockport, e-reward

XpertHR (2013) How to select, devise, and use a job evaluation scheme [Online] http://www.xperthr.co.uk/how-to/how-to-select-devise-and-use-a-job-evaluation-scheme/155642/ [accessed 30 September 2017]

APPENDIX A
Job evaluation glossary

Analytical job evaluation A job evaluation technique in which whole jobs are broken down into a number of defined elements or factors such as responsibility, decisions and the knowledge and skill required. These are assumed to be present in all the jobs to be evaluated.

Analytical matching Jobs are analysed into a number of factors and matched either to grade profiles or benchmark jobs which have been set out under the same factor headings.

Benchmark job A typical job that represents the different occupations and levels of work in an organization and is used as a point of reference with which other jobs can be compared and evaluated.

Comparable worth Work of equal value.

Factor A criterion for judging the value of a job in one particular element or characteristic of the work involved, for example, skill, responsibility, complexity. It is assumed that this element is present in all the jobs to be evaluated. It is also assumed that the elements will be present in jobs to different degrees that can be measured on a points scale or by reference to grade or level definitions.

Factor comparison scheme The original factor comparison method compared jobs factor by factor using a scale of money values to provide a direct indication of the rate for the job. It was developed in the United States but is not used in the UK. A revised version is used in the United States which resembles a conventional point-factor scheme except that there are no level definitions. Jobs are simply placed on a scale for each factor.

Factor plan A definition of the group of factors that are used in a point-factor job evaluation scheme. The individual factors will be divided into defined levels and the total points that can be allocated to a factor are assigned and distributed between each level. The allocation of points may be weighted in accordance with judgements about the relative importance of each factor.

Graduated factor comparison Jobs are compared with one another factor by factor with a graduated scale. The scale may have only three value levels – for example lower, equal, higher – and no factor scores are used.

Job analysis The process of collecting, analysing and setting out information about the content of jobs in order to provide the basis for a job description.

Job classification (job grading) A non-analytical method of job evaluation that allocates jobs into grades by comparing the whole job with a scale in the form of a hierarchy of grade definitions.

Job description A definition of the main tasks that are involved in carrying out the job. For job evaluation purposes it is usual to include an analysis of the job in terms of the criteria used in a factor plan.

Job evaluation A systematic process for establishing the relative worth of jobs within an organization.

Job evaluation scheme A structured approach to job evaluation that specifies systematic procedures for analysing jobs and criteria for assessing the size of individual jobs and for comparing jobs with one another.

Job matching The comparison of one job with another job or other jobs to determine internal relativities. Job matching can be done analytically (ie by reference to the common factors or elements assumed to be present in all jobs) or non-analytically (ie for whole jobs without reference to their factors or elements).

Job size In point-factor or factor comparison job evaluation schemes, the value of the job as indicated by its points score.

Job slotting Placing a job in a grade or band by reference to grade definitions which have not been analysed into factors, sometimes called non-analytical matching.

Levelling A method of job evaluation which focuses on defining the levels of work in an organization and fitting jobs into those levels. It can simply be an alternative term for job classification.

Market pricing The process of analysing market rates to establish external relativities and provide a guide to the development of a competitive pay structure, ie one in which levels of pay enable the organization to attract and retain the talented people it needs. Extreme market pricing involves relying entirely on market rate data to establish internal relativities.

Non-analytical job evaluation scheme Whole jobs that have not been analysed by reference to their elements or factors are compared in order to place.

Point-factor rating Jobs are scored by reference to a set of factors in a factor plan in order to determine their relative size.

Weighting The process in a point-factor scheme of varying the points available for each of the factors according to assumptions about their relative importance (explicit weighting) or by allocating more levels to some factors than others (implicit weighting).

APPENDIX B
Point-factor job evaluation scheme

Factor plan

Factor	Levels				
	1	**2**	**3**	**4**	**5**
1 Knowledge and skills (general)	30	60	90	120	150
2 Interpersonal skills	15	30	45	60	75
3 Judgement and decision making	20	40	60	80	100
4 Complexity	15	30	45	60	75
5 Responsibility for resources	20	40	60	80	100

Factor and level definitions

1. Knowledge and skills (general)

The level of professional, specialist, technical, administrative or operational knowledge and expertise required to carry out the role effectively

1 The use of the skills required to carry out straightforward work.

2 The application of specific administrative or technical skills.

3 The application of a range of professional, specialist, technical, administrative or operational areas of knowledge and skills.

4 The application of high levels of professional, specialist, technical or administrative expertise.

5 The application of authoritative expertise in a key area of the organization's activities.

2. Interpersonal skills

The level of skill required to work well with others, to respond to people's requests, to handle difficult cases, to argue a case, to negotiate and to exert influence

1 Requires the skills to work well with others and respond politely and competently to requests and enquiries.

2 Requires the skills to exert some influence over others, getting them to accept a proposal or point of view.

3 Requires the skills to frequently relate to people inside and outside the organization, providing advice and guidance, dealing with problems affecting people and exerting influence on important matters. The skills may be used in negotiations and joint problem solving on relatively straightforward issues.

4 Requires the skills to constantly relate to people at senior levels inside and outside the organization on non-routine issues, providing advice and guidance internally on the interpretation and application of company policies.

5 Requires the skills to deal with internal and external contacts at high levels, handling important and non-routine issues and involving the exercise of considerable persuasive ability, sensitivity to others and tact. The skills may be used when conducting important negotiations, dealing with difficult and sensitive cases or acting as the recognized representative of the company on key issues externally.

3. Judgement and decision making

The requirement to exercise judgement in making decisions and solving problems, including the degree to which the work involves choice of action and the extent to which the job holder is free to act

1 The work is well-defined and relatively few new situations are encountered. The causes of problems are readily identifiable and can be dealt with easily.

2 Evaluation of information is required to deal with occasional new problems and situations and to decide on a course of action from known alternatives. Specific guidelines exist on what needs to be done and the more complex problems are referred to a higher authority.

3 Exercises discriminating judgement in dealing with relatively new or unusual problems where a wide range of information has to be considered and the courses of action are not immediately obvious. Takes independent action within defined policy frameworks.

(continued)

4   Frequently exercises independent judgement when faced with unusual problems and situations where no policy guidelines or precedents are available.

5   Deals on own initiative with widely differing problems calling for extreme clarity of thought in assessing conflicting information and balancing the risks associated with possible solutions.

4. Complexity

The variety and diversity of the work carried out, the decisions to be made and the knowledge and skills used

1   Work requirements are on the whole well-defined and involve a fairly limited range of activities.

2   There is some diversity in the work which involves a number of non-routine elements and the exercise of a variety of skills although they are quite closely related to one another.

3   The work is diverse, consisting of a number of different elements which are only broadly related to one another and the exercise of a wide variety of skills.

4   The work is highly diverse, involving many different elements which may not be closely related to one another.

5   The work is multi-disciplinary and involves making a broad range of highly diverse decisions.

5. Responsibility for resources

The size of the resources controlled in terms of people, money, equipment, facilities etc

1   Responsible only for the equipment required to carry out the work.

2   May have two or three staff reporting to him or her, and/or monitors expenditure.

3   May lead a small team, and/or manage a small budget or be responsible for a range of facilities or equipment.

4   Leads a large team or department of more than 10 people, and/or acts as budget manager for a department or office.

5   Leads a major function or range of activities and manages a commensurately sized budget.

APPENDIX C
Example of a job questionnaire

Basic Details	
Job Title:	**Name(s) of job holder(s):**
Department:	

Reporting Structure

1 Please fill in the job titles of:

- Your line manager _____

- Your department manager (if different) _____

- People who you line manage (if applicable) _____

Job

Overall purpose of job

2 Describe as concisely as possible the overall purpose of your job – what in general terms you are expected to achieve. (You may find this at the top of your job description).

As an alternative to completing the rest of this section you may wish to attach your job description if it accurately reflects what you do. Or you can attach the job description and provide some extra information below if you think this will help the evaluators to understand your role.

Main activities

3 List the main activities you carry out. All jobs can be described in a relatively small number of key headings – not more than eight. Do not describe the activity in detail – one sentence to explain its essential nature will do. If you think it would be helpful to get a better understanding of your job, give an indication of what time you spend on each part of your job (as a percentage of the total).

(continued)

Scope

4 Describe the extent to which your work is guided by guidelines, procedures or precedents and on what kinds of activities your job requires you to make choices.

5 Describe how regularly and on what your job requires supervision, giving examples of the kinds of things you typically receive or ask guidance on from your manager.

6 Give examples of the actions, advice and decisions you are free to make without needing guidance or approval from anyone else.

7 Does your job involve you in adapting procedures or finding new ways of working to improve how things are done, either in your own area of work or through participation in/leadership of project teams? Give examples.

8 Give examples of what you have to plan for/prioritize in your work, either for yourself or for others – and what timescale this typically covers.

Impact of decisions (this is about when work is being done to the required standard, not about the consequences of things going wrong)

9 Give examples of how the actions, recommendations and decisions that you take impact on any of the following:

- Day-to-day operations in your area of work or elsewhere in the organization.

- Colleagues/volunteers in your own area of work, or elsewhere in the organization.

- Clients, customers or other external contacts/bodies.

- External perception or reputation of the organization.

*In giving examples, please give an indication of the **risks and benefits** that are taken into account and the **timescale** over which your actions, recommendations and decisions take effect.*

Resources

10 Describe what resources or assets you are directly responsible for, eg planning, allocating or spending budgets, equipment (including equipment you use on a day-to-day basis), premises, or raising income.

11 If applicable, quantify the resource(s) involved, eg budget/quantity.

12 Do you have any other responsibility for resources that you are not directly accountable for, eg monitoring resource usage (such as records of monies, people or equipment), ensuring their safe-keeping, or in generating or spending income? If so, please describe.

(continued)

Interpersonal skills

13 Please complete the following table to describe the key people or groups of people that you have to work with in your job, excluding the colleagues in your own department that you work with on a day-to-day basis. Include internal and external contacts.

Who (individuals or organizations)	Frequency	Purpose

16 How many people, if any, do you manage?

A. Directly _____

B. Indirectly (ie report in through others) _____

C. Not applicable _____

(Note: This answer should tie into the section on reporting structure.)

17 If applicable, describe to what extent are their jobs similar or dissimilar (to each other and to your own), and where they are based.

18 If there are colleagues/volunteers that do not report to you, but for whom you supervise/direct work, provide guidance or are involved in their development, please state who this is for, and what it involves.

Applied knowledge and skills (this is about what is needed to be able to do the job – this may not be the same as your own personal experience or background)

19 What are the basic skills, whether acquired inside or outside the organization, that are needed to do your job?

20 Are any specific professional, technical or vocational skills or qualifications required to do the job?

21 On what kinds of things do other people come to you for information, advice or as a source of expertise, because of the kind of knowledge and skills that your role requires you to have? Give examples – whether inside the organization or externally.

22 If your role requires you to be the sole or main source of knowledge or expertise in a particular field of work, describe what this covers.

(continued)

Your comments: is there anything else about your job, not covered by the questions above, which will help others to understand and evaluate your job?

Thank you for completing this questionnaire

Before sending the completed questionnaire to HR, job holders and line managers should both read the verification statement and confirm the accuracy of the information provided by entering the date, as requested.

Verification statement	
I/we agree that this completed questionnaire accurately reflects the requirements of the job	
Name of manager	**Date questionnaire contents confirmed by line manager**
	/ /
	Date questionnaire contents confirmed by job holder(s)
	/ /

INDEX

ACAS 1, 5, 6
analytical job evaluation schemes
    14–15, 184
analytical levelling job evaluation
    schemes 14
analytical matching job evaluation
    schemes
    characteristics, advantages and
        disadvantages 42
    combined with point-factor
        rating 18, 99–100
    defined 14
    described 99
    grade profiles 107–08
    job-to-grade 99–100
    job-to-job 100
appeals procedure 55–56
assimilation policy 57–58, 165

Babcock, L 152
benchmark jobs
    and analytical matching 100
    defined 13
    evaluation of 85–86, 87
    and grade profiles 107
    and grade structure design 163
    and market pricing 145–46
    profiles 102–03
    selection of 84–85
    use in testing 87
benchmarking 15
broad-banded 14, 141, 158
broad-graded 158, 166
Brown, D 1, 133–34, 138, 152, 166,
    183, 184, 185

capsule job description 145
career path 108
CIPD 141
comparable worth 15
computer-aided job analysis 56
computer-aided job evaluation
    case against 25
    case for 21–22, 24

defined 20
types of 21
methodology 20–21, 23
and paper schemes 88–89

decision band method of job
    evaluation 135–37
decision-making accountability
    (DMA) method of job evaluation
    137–39
derived market rate 152
developing job evaluation schemes
    communicating to employees 51
    designing a point-factor
        scheme 78–88
    the development programme 45–51
    practical guidance 51–55
    procedures and policies 55–58
Dewey, J 6
Differentials 164
Dive, B 134, 137, 138, 183
DMA (decision-making accountability)
    method of job evaluation 134,
    137–39
Dworschak, B 152

Ellis, C M 11, 149
Emerson, S M 9
Employment Tribunals 15
equal pay
    defending a equal pay claim 171–
        72
    and equitable pay 5
    and job evaluation 169, 175–76
    managing the risk of equal pay
        claims 172–74
    reviews 174–75
equitable pay 5
e-reward 1–2, 73, 75, 161, 179,
    185–86
explicit weighting 71, 75, 83–84
external relativities 1, 142
extreme market pricing 11, 29, 32, 36,
    142–43, 151

factor comparison job evaluation
    schemes 14–15
factor plan 72, 73–74, 75–76, 82, 84,
    85, 86–87
factor weighting 74–75
factors, job evaluation 9, 72–73,
    85–86
Findlay, J 152
focus group 79
formal job evaluation schemes 1,
    10–11, 13–18, 19, 27–29, 31–32,
    36
Friends Provident 109–11

genetic role profiles 109
grade definitions 112–13
grade and pay structures
    broad-banded 14
    defined 157
    defining grades 159
    development of 157–67
    and non-analytical matching 100
    types of 158
grade profile 107–08, 114–17
grade structures
    defined 7, 99, 157–58
    defining grades 159
    design of 103, 159–61
    grades within levels 166
    and matching schemes 102
    types of 158
graduated factor comparison 15
Gupta, N 6

Hay Guide Chart job evaluation
    method 9, 19, 129
hierarchy 8

implicit weighting 71, 79, 84
independent experts 15
individual job range 141, 158, 166
informal job evaluation 1, 20, 29,
    32–33
Institute for Employment Studies 1,
    183, 184
internal benchmarking 16
internal equity 7, 151, 152
internal market 7
internal relativities 1
intrinsic value 6

Jaques, E 5, 144–45
Jenkins, G D 6
job analysis
    computer-aided job analysis 56
    conducting a job analysis
        interview 61–65
    defined 59
    parties involved 66–67
    role profile 59, 60
    structured interviews 59–60
    written questionnaire 65–66
job classification 16, 99
job content 7
job description 59, 99, 145
job elements 72
job evaluation
    analytical job evaluation
        schemes 14–15, 99–100
    analytical matching schemes 14
    appeals procedure 55–56
    choice of approach 35–43
    combined approaches 18–19
    computer-aided job evaluation 20–25
    criteria for choice 38–39
    decision-making accountability
        (DMA) method of job
        evaluation 137–39
    defined 1, 5, 142
    and design of job family
        structures 161–62
    developing job evaluation
        schemes 45–58
    and equal pay 169, 175–76
    factor comparison job evaluation
        schemes 14–15
    factor levels 80–82
    factor plan 73–74, 75–76
    factors 9, 72–73
    features of 8–10
    formal schemes 1, 10–11, 13–20,
        27–29, 31–32, 36, 38–43
    graduated factor comparison 15
    incidence of 1–2
    informal job evaluation 1, 20, 29,
        32–33, 36, 38
    internal benchmarking 16
    job classification 16, 99
    job ranking 17
    levelling 14, 43, 133–39
    maintain job evaluation 179–82

and market pricing 142
matching job evaluation schemes,
9, 99–100
methodology 10–11, 13–25
non-analytical job evaluation
schemes 15–18
non-analytical matching 16, 10,
100–01
objectives 33, 36
off-the-shelf (ready-made) job
evaluation schemes 19–20, 40
paired comparison ranking 15,
17–18
point-factor schemes 14, 18, 19,
42, 71–76
points 6
proprietary brands of job
evaluation 19, 40
purpose of 5–6
ready-made schemes 19–20, 40
reviewing job evaluation 27–34
schemes 80–82, 142
scoring progression, point-factor
job evaluation scheme 75–76
specification for scheme 33–34
tailor-made job evaluation schemes
19, 40
use of schemes 25
weighting, job evaluation
factors 74–75
job evaluation factors
categories of 72–73
defined 9, 72
levels 80–82
most frequently used 73
selection and design of 77–80
variations in 73
job evaluation schemes
defined 142
levels 80–82
and market pricing 142
job evaluation schemes, development
of, *see* developing job evaluation
job family defined 108, 129
job family modelling (Hay
Group) 129–31
job family structures 108, 118–20,
158, 161–62
job profile 99, 103–07, 145
job-to-grade evaluation (matching) 15,
100, 159–60

job-to-job evaluation (matching) 15,
99–100
job matching, market rate
analysis 144–45
job ranking 17
job size 6, 9
job slotting 99, 101, and 185
jobs 8

labour theory of value 7
level profiles 107
level structure, *see* grade structure
levelling
characteristics, advantages and
disadvantages 43
defined 14, 133
grades within levels 166
and grade structure design 159–60
and matching 99
use of 185
levels, job evaluation schemes 80–82

market-driven 143
market grouping 158, 166
market pay levels 146
market pricing
application of 142–43
defined 141
extreme market pricing 11, 29, 32,
36, 142–43
and job evaluation 1, 142
limitations of 150–53
market rate analysis 143–50
market rate surveys 143, 147–49
and market value 7, 8
requirements for 143–44
use of 11, 141
market rate 141, 142, 150–51
market rate analysis
job matching 144–45
process of 145–50
requirements for 143–45
market rate comparisons 1, 7
market rate data, sources of 146–50
market rate surveys 143, 147–49
market reference points 163
market stance 163
market value 7–8
market worth 8, 151
matching job evaluation schemes
defined 9, 99

development of 101–25
job-to-grade analytical
    matching 99–100
job-to-job analytical matching 100
matching procedure 108, 121
non-analytical matching 100–01
Marx, K 7
mid-point (pay range) 166
multi-graded structures, 158, 163–65
Munday, S 133–34, 185

narrow-graded structures 158
Nielson, N H 7
NHS 126–29
non-analytical job evaluation
    schemes 15–18, 43
non-analytical matching 16
Novartis 138–39

off-the-shelf (tailor-made) job
    evaluation schemes 19–20
overlap (pay ranges or grades) 165

paired comparison ranking 15, 17–18
Paterson, T T 134, 135–37
pay differentials 164
pay range
    mid-point 166
    overlap 165
    practice point 163
    reference point 163, 164, 165
pay spines 158
pay structures
    defined 7, 162
    development of 162–63
Pilat 25
Plachy, R J 10
point-factor rating job evaluation
    schemes
    characteristics, advantages and
        disadvantages 42
    combined with analytical
        matching 18
    combined with non-analytical
        matching 19
    defined 14
    design of 76–88
    example of 189–96
    factor levels 71, 80–82
    factor plan 72, 73–74, 75–76, 82,
        84, 85, 86–87
    factors 9, 72–73

and grade design 160–61
and grade structure design 160–61
job evaluation factors 72–73
and levelling 133–34
methodology 71–76
points 72
scoring 72, 82
scoring progression 71–72, 75–76,
    82
trends 184
use of 71
weighting job evaluation
    factors 74–75, 82–84
practice point 163
proprietary (consultants') brands of
    job evaluation 13, 19, 40
protection policy 56, 165

reference point 163, 164, 165, 166
relative value 7
role profile 59, 60, 99

Schmidt, W 152
Schuster, J R 142–43
scoring progression, point-factor job
    evaluation scheme 71–72, 75–76
size of jobs 6, 9
slotting 99, 101
spot rates 141, 158
structured interviews 59–60
Sygenta 122–26

tailor-made job evaluation schemes 19,
    40
target rate 163
Tesco 138
time span of discretion 134–35

Unilever 138

value 6–8
Vodafone 138

weighting, job evaluation factors
    74–75, 82–84
WorldatWork 146
worth 6

XpertHR 1, 141, 183

Zingheim, P K 142–43